We

Welcome to the Christian Faith

Christopher L. Webber

Morehouse Publishing
NEW YORK · HARRISBURG · DENVER

The Scripture quotations contained herein are from the New Revised Standard Version Bible, copyright © 1989 by the Division of Christian Education of the National Council of Churches of Christ in the U.S.A. Used by permission. All rights reserved.

Morehouse Publishing
4775 Linglestown Road, Harrisburg, PA 17112

Morehouse Publishing
445 Fifth Avenue, New York, NY 10016

Morehouse Publishing is an imprint of
Church Publishing Incorporated
www.churchpublishing.org

Series cover design by Corey Kent

Library of Congress Cataloging-in-Publication Data
Webber, Christopher.
  Welcome to the Christian faith / Christopher L. Webber.
    p.   cm.
  ISBN 978-0-8192-2743-0 (pbk.)—ISBN 978-0-8192-2744-7
  (ebook)
  1. Christianity. 2. Theology, Doctrinal—Popular works. I. Title.
BT77.W43 2011
230—dc23

                                                    2011020038

Printed in the United States of America

Contents

Preface

Some two thousand years ago, a man named Jesus was born in a small town in an unimportant part of the great Roman Empire. When he had grown up, he began a ministry of teaching and healing that briefly seems to have created great excitement, but the authorities had him arrested and killed. That might have been the end of the story, but the small group of followers he had trained began to tell others that in knowing this Jesus they had come to know God in a new and life-changing way. They also said that although Jesus had truly died, he had also been restored to life by the power of God and that they continued to know him in a deep and personal way. They called others to join them in this experience of faith and to tell others about the way of life that was soon being called "Christianity."

Now, nearly two thousand years later, this Jesus continues to be a living reality for millions of people in every part of the world. Every day, others come to ask about this faith and whether it will transform their lives as well. Every day, still others who grew up as Christians but never really asked themselves what that might mean come seeking a deeper understanding of what Christian faith might mean for them.

This book has been written in the hope that God can speak through it to those who are looking for a deeper understanding of the mysteries of life and faith. When this search for understanding is coupled with membership in a Christian congregation, with Bible study, and with prayer, lives can be changed through a living relationship with that Jesus who lives still today and who calls us to help renew the world. No book can answer all the questions that might be asked. Christianity, in any event, is "caught, not taught." Simply providing answers can never turn an inquirer into a believer. But it may help. Certainly having better answers can help open the door to a living faith.

Some who have read this book have suggested that it might begin with the chapter about Jesus, since he is so central to Christian faith. Readers should feel free to begin with that chapter—or any other, for that matter, that most interests them. This is not a novel that needs to be read in sequence, but a set of answers, or partial answers—there are no complete answers!—to questions that might be asked. Feel free to explore these topics in whatever order makes sense to you.

Believing

BELIEVING IS A VERB

Who is God? Who am I?

One of the first words a child learns to say is, "Why?" Other animals, so far as we can tell, never ask that. They are what they are and they do what they do. Life, for them, is not complicated. Human beings, on the other hand, feel a need to know, to understand why we are here and how we should therefore act.

The American folksinger Odetta sang a lullaby that went, "Why and why and why and why; why and why and why," and continued, "Because, because, because, because; good night, good night!" Parents do get tired of having to explain everything and sometimes children get tired of asking. We all can get tired of asking our questions, and simply accept the statement we heard as children, "That's just the way it is." That's unfortunate. We were designed to ask and look for answers and the search for answers leads us finally to issues of faith.

Many questions, of course, have simple, logical answers:

"Why should I eat my spinach?"

1

"You should eat your spinach so you will get your vitamins and grow strong."

Other questions can be answered by scientific investigation:

"Why are there stars?"
"There are stars because there was an enormous explosion thirteen or fourteen billion years ago that produced clouds of energy that formed the stars and galaxies and planets.

"Why does water boil?"
"Water boils because heat causes the liquid to expand and turn into steam."

All this is useful, but leaves the ultimate "why" questions still unanswered. To say that I am here because a male and female united to produce a child is true enough as far as it goes, but it doesn't go far enough for most of us.

WHY BELIEVE?
Why are we here? Is the world just a random collision of atoms, or is there a plan and a purpose to it all? Science has no answers to that kind of question, leading some to think that means there *are* no answers, nor is there any plan or purpose; that everything we see is the result of a random chain of events. But the lack of a scientific answer does not necessarily mean that there are no answers. A lot of the decisions and commitments we make are and always have been "unscientific." I will decide to become a farmer rather than a doctor, or a computer programmer rather than a stock broker, because something deep within leads me in that direction. I could go to a guidance counselor and take tests that would give me a more scientific basis for my choice, but most of us will let our own instincts guide us. So, too, in committing myself to another person in marriage, I could—

and should—seek counseling and perhaps take personality tests to look for compatibility factors, but the final decision—and the success of that commitment—will still come from somewhere deep within that leads me to believe that this is right for me. We *believe* and therefore we act.

But *why* do we believe? Here we are on very different ground than a scientist would be. The scientist is curious and conducts experiments to see what happens and why it happens. She applies heat to water and notices that it boils. She does it again with the same result. When it continues to happen, she proposes a theory: "Heated water boils." Other scientists can then test her theory by repeating the experiment. Believing is not like that. Believing, first of all, is personal: it's not about a stove and a pot of water. It's about me, and about what I choose to do. Why do I choose to believe?

BELIEVING IS ABOUT RELATIONSHIPS

"Believe" is a verb, and a verb usually has both a subject and an object. Believing is something human beings do, and it has an object because believing is about a *relationship*. Sometimes, of course, we use the verb "believe" to express a hunch or an informed guess. We say things like, "I believe it will rain tomorrow." But that is not really believing. Believing has to do with confidence in someone: that they are real and can be trusted in a relationship. That sort of believing is based on instinct and experience.

Still, there is something more involved. We seem to have a need for such relationships. Human beings, the scientists would say, are "social animals"; we tend to form communities and work together toward common goals. In that shared life, we are idealists. We look for people who have skills and qualities that seem to enrich our lives. Most people eventually form an exclusive relationship with another who seems to embody our highest ideals. Yet, if we are honest, we know that we are always disappointed to some degree. Whether partners or presidents, we learn again and again that the other is also human. We have an unsatisfied yearning for something more.

In the early years of the Christian church, a man named Augustine said that God has made us to be in relationship with God, and "our hearts are restless" until they find rest in that relationship. More recently, the French philosopher Blaise Pascal said that each person has an emptiness in the heart that they try in vain to fill; in other words, there is an emptiness within us that requires a relationship with God to be satisfied. We cannot, by definition, prove that such a psychological need exists. We have only our own experience to guide us, but most people do have such a longing.

Many people, of course, will deny that they have such a longing, even when it is obvious through their actions that they are trying to satisfy some kind of need. We see billionaires trying to make more billions, computer owners trying to move up to the latest technology, and parents trying to get their children into the best schools. There are even those who are constantly trying to find new and better techniques of meditation. Our hearts do, indeed, seem restless and unsatisfied. Perhaps what we are really seeking is a relationship with God to satisfy that innate human need.

But if we do have such a need for a relationship with God, does it necessarily follow that we want to believe in God—or would we prefer to know who this God is in some empirical or scientific way? Isn't one result of a world dominated (and threatened!) by scientific achievement a feeling that everything worthwhile is gained by testing and proving so that we know? When we talk about God and the ultimate purpose of life, surely this is an area where we would like to be sure?

In Ingmar Bergman's movie *The Seventh Seal,* a medieval knight, anguished by doubt, is the central figure. He cries out at one point in the movie, "What is going to happen to those of us who want to believe but aren't able to? . . . Why can't I kill God within me? Why does He live on in this painful and humiliating way even though I curse Him and want to tear Him out of my heart? Why, in spite of everything, is He a baffling reality that I can't shake off?"

That feeling is more modern than medieval. We often look back at the Middle Ages as an "age of faith" and look at our own world as one in which matters of faith are increasingly pushed aside. Yet for all the abundance of material things with which our lives are filled, we seem less satisfied than ever. The medieval mind, less dominated by the achievements of science, could more easily take God's existence for granted while we, who know so much about the universe and live in a world where God seems absent, are more likely to question.

There are, in fact, several ways to answer "the God question." In the first place, if we are investigating Christianity, we are talking about a living relationship, and science has very few certain answers to provide in that sphere. A marriage counselor can analyze the answers to a "compatibility" test, but there no guarantees available that the marriage will work. Parents would like to do the best things for their children, but science can provide no certain answers about what those "best things" are for each individual child. When we talk about the relationship between God and a human being, we are likely to find even less certainty.

In the second place, what would love be like if it were based on certainties? Isn't mystery an important part of the love relationship? Can you imagine being in love with someone whose responses were always predictable?

In the third place, who are we to expect to understand the ultimate power in the universe? Few of us can really understand even Einstein's general theory of relativity, and here we are discussing something far beyond that. Who are you, God asked Job, to speak to your Creator? "Shall a faultfinder contend with the Almighty?" (Job 40:2).

Two Kinds of Knowing

Given, then, our human limitations, we might begin with this question: "What can we know and how do we know it?" We hear a great deal about the "conflict" between science and religion. But there is no need for a conflict if each respects the realm of the other. A scientist, in fact, will often proceed in faith in the early stages of a project. She believes she is on the right track and tests to prove it. In matters of religion, on the other hand, we are right to proceed by reason and logic as far as we can. We may need at last to act in faith when we have gone beyond what can be tested and demonstrated, but we should not assume science has nothing to teach us or that our minds can be left outside when we go into a church.

Believing is, however, a different way of knowing. Our minds work in ways that are far from fully understood to gain experience and produce sudden insights. Poets and other writers talk about the way their pens (or word processors) produce thoughts they had not known they had until they began to write. They sometimes use the word "revelation" to describe a sudden and unexpected insight that seems to come from outside themselves. Much of the Bible is that kind of writing. The prophets spoke words that came to them "in the spirit." The words were not theirs, but came to them even in spite of themselves. Christians speak of the Bible as "revealed truth" because so much of it comes from that sort of unexpected and unpredictable insight. (The chapter on the Bible will discuss this further.)

In fact, scientists also sometimes proceed by revelation. Einstein spoke of the dreams in which he first came to understand some new aspect of the laws of physics. The human mind works in ways beyond our present understanding to produce these insights or revelations, some of which can later be tested and verified and others of which are not that same kind of truth. Revelations can also, in some cases, be tested and verified by experience, but that is a different kind of proof.

Two aspects of human life seem to be especially involved in this kind of knowledge: an awareness of our failures, and our sense of wonder. It is generally when we think about ourselves that we are struck with an awareness of our failures, and when we think about the created order outside ourselves that we are filled with awe. These may in fact, however, be two sides of the same phenomenon. A great German scholar, Rudolf Otto, spoke of our sense of "creatureliness." That sense of "creatureliness" cuts both ways; it involves a sense of our littleness in the great expanse of the universe that makes us say both "How great Thou art" and also "I repent."

Awe and wonder

The story is told of a bishop who fell into conversation with a man who said, much like Ingmar Bergman's knight, that he wanted a revelation. "Go outside," said the bishop, "on a rainy night and turn your face to the heavens and perhaps something will come to you." Sometime later they met again and the bishop asked whether the man had tried the experiment. "Yes," said the man. "I went outside on a rainy night and turned my face to the sky and the rain ran down my neck and I felt like a fool." "Well," said the bishop, "that's not bad for a first revelation."

The sense of God's greatness and our weakness and fool-
ishness are, indeed, closely linked. But it may be best to
begin with God's greatness and the human sense of wonder.
Like the question "why?" the sense of wonder is strongest in
children. Adults often begin to think that they have "been
there, done that" and seen it all before, and so they lose their
ability to gaze in wonder not only at the night sky but even
at a grain of sand or blade of grass. The wise rabbi Nachman
of Breslov once said, "It is forbidden to be old.... For the
child knows how to be amazed, everything to him is new—
the sky, the sun, the stars, mother, father, the doll. He par-
ticipates in the biblical statement, 'And God saw everything
that He had made and it was very good.' Adults, unfortunately, have ceased to be astounded. They see no mystery;
freshness is hidden under names and categories."

To say that our sense of wonder is produced by our awareness of the magnitude of creation and our inability to comprehend so vast a universe is true, but far from the whole
story. If it were, it would be rather like the inability of my
desktop computer to do the calculations involved in launch-
ing a lunar probe. My computer can't handle it, perhaps, but
a bigger computer can. The job can be done. Gazing at the
night sky, however, whether with the naked eye or the most
powerful telescope, is something else again. Perhaps a computer could be imagined with enough processing power to
calculate the range and motion of all the objects out there,
but something more seems to be involved. We have to ask
whether at last there is a reality that cannot be measured because it is literally immeasurable.

In somewhat the same way, it is certainly possible for me
to analyze and even duplicate the lines drawn by Picasso or
the pigments employed by Rembrandt, but gazing at Picasso's
Guernica or Rembrandt's *Descent from the Cross* is not simply
a matter of analyzing or even comprehending the materials

involved. I see such works of art and I respond in a way beyond any analysis. I can come back to see them again and again and still learn from them, be moved by them, be challenged and transformed by them. "Awe" and "wonder" are words we use to describe a way of knowing that is real and valid, although far beyond testing and measurement. Any adequate analysis of human life must be able to include those aspects of our experience that are real and that enrich our lives in ways beyond scientific analysis.

Sin

Sin is another subject that must be dealt with more fully later, but it is often—some would say always—an experience that leads to believing. The same vision that looks out at the universe and responds with awe also turns around to look at the self, and responds not simply with a quite inevitable sense of littleness, but also with a sense of moral failure.

Why does morality come into this picture? The sense of awe may be reduced to a simple matter of scale: the universe is so large and we are so small. But the sense of sinfulness is not a matter of scale, of large and small, but of value—and this involves a totally different type of measurement. If a scientist produces inaccurate data, we will look at his results and judge them to be wrong. We might say that the one who produced these figures is a bad scientist, but if the data has been deliberately falsified, we will then say that the scientist is a bad person—and that is a very different matter. What is it that leads us to make such judgments?

The moral sense may, in fact, be easier for a scientist to explain than the sense of wonder. It has survival value. If the members of a tribe can be imbued with a sense of right and wrong, they are more likely to work together in a harmonious fashion; they will be less prone to steal their neighbor's chunk of dinosaur meat or claim the wheel as their own invention

when, in fact, it was not theirs. But these would be sins
against the social fabric and could be dealt with by a system
of fines and other punishments created by the tribe for its
own welfare. What we find, however, in human societies
everywhere is a sense that such misbehavior is not only a
crime but a "sin," an offense against a moral law created by
a higher power. Primitive societies have developed a variety
of elaborate rituals for placating this power or these powers,
including sacrificial offerings that are made to restore har-
mony not simply, or even primarily, within the human community, but with a spiritual world beyond.

The value of life

The evidence of a moral sense brings us one step closer to
an intuition of life that goes beyond the vegetable and animal
life with which we are surrounded, and leads to a belief that
life is not simply an aspect of material existence. If I have of-
fended a power beyond myself, that power also may possess
life, a life that is not dependent on the physical or material
life of the body. Further, if there is a higher power that is in
some sense beyond time or eternal, the life I have here on
earth for a span of years may also extend beyond that span
in some way. The fact that grave offerings have been found
in Neanderthal burial sites would indicate that this intuition
of life extending in some form beyond death has come at a
very early stage of human history.

WHAT DO WE KNOW AND
HOW DO WE KNOW IT?

Let's come back again to the questions of what we know and
how we know it. This discussion of awe and sin and life is
not intended to "prove" anything, but only to explore why it
is that we tend to ask "why?" They are what one writer has
called "a rumor of angels": indications that there is "something

out there" and questions that need answers beyond those that can be supplied by testing and verification.

Christians have wrestled with these questions over the centuries, and so have members of other religious systems. Nearly a thousand years ago, one of the greatest Christian theologians, Thomas Aquinas, suggested five arguments, or "proofs," for the existence of God. Other theologians and philosophers, of course, have disputed the value of these arguments, but it remains worthwhile to look at some of them and see what value they might have for us today.

1. The First Cause

Think, for example, about existence itself and the fact that we live on an inhabitable world in a vast universe. How did that happen? Why are we here? Why is there *something* and not *nothing*? Scientists may talk about the "Big Bang" that set it all in motion, but what created the Big Bang? What was here before that?

One of the most obvious rules of life is that something does not come from nothing. Nothing happens without a cause. Creation cannot happen without a Creator.

A common instinct when children are first confronted with this problem is to say, "But who created the Creator?"—and we can continue to ask that question indefinitely. Our nearest experience of eternity may be a long and boring sermon or, it is sometimes said, the leftover turkey from Thanksgiving Day dinner. This is not, however, really very long, nor is the span of human life—nor, when you come down to it, is the time life has existed on this planet when measured against the time from the Big Bang until now. Yet all of these timeframes are still measurable, and we are being asked to deal with what cannot be measured. Since we have no experience of such a thing, our minds find it hard to imagine an uncreated existence or an eternal being. But our minds have no alternative. Living as we do in a world where every effect has a cause, our minds are not prepared to conceive of another possibility. "God," then, is one solution to the problem. Given a choice between a Creator—a "First Cause"—and an infinite series of random causes, we tend to prefer the idea of an eternally existing Creator.

But what does this solution really "prove"? It demonstrates, for one thing, the limits of our human minds. But why should we expect our minds to be able to answer all questions and understand everything? While I may not understand Einstein's theory of relativity other minds may, and the theory may be true whether I understand it or not. So also there may be a solution to the problem of creation that my mind cannot comprehend.

The possible existence of a First Cause also tells us nothing about the nature of that Cause. The Cause might be personal or impersonal, benevolent or evil. Perhaps the character is right in Shakespeare's play *King Lear* who says:

As flies to wanton boys, are we to the gods.
They kill us for their sport.

So we cannot say that our existence "proves" a Creator, but the question of why there is something and not nothing must at least make us thoughtful. It seems not unreasonable to suggest that existence implies a Cause and that the God Christians and others speak of may be that Cause.

2. The Evidence of Design
Somewhat different from the argument from the need for a Creator is the argument from the evidence of design. Theologians point out that when we find a watch lying on the street we assume there was a watchmaker. Watches don't just happen; someone skillful makes them. In the same way, if

we look around at the complexity and order of nature, we might well assume that its existence is not purely accidental.

The theory of evolution goes a long way, of course, toward explaining the diversity and complexity of life. If forms of life evolve to fill niches in the potential tapestry of life, that may explain why oak trees produce acorns and squirrels evolve to eat them while banana trees produce bananas and monkeys evolve to eat them. Meanwhile, of course, foxes evolve to eat squirrels and jaguars evolve to eat monkeys, while oak trees evolve to produce more acorns than squirrels can eat and vultures evolve to eat what the foxes and jaguars leave behind. Nevertheless, scientists and amateur bird watchers alike find the same sense of awe for the beauty and diversity of nature arising at the sight of a soaring hawk, a leaping porpoise, the infinite variety of birds at a backyard bird feeder, or the stars shining in the night sky. Some scientists have suggested that the forces in the physical universe are so precisely balanced that it is hard to imagine it is pure coincidence.

As with the idea that creation implies a Creator, the suggestion that the appearance of design in the universe implies a Designer tells us little about the nature of that Designer. What kind of Designer would include volcanoes and hurricanes in the design and create human beings so prone to violence?

Some Christians have attempted to take a form of the argument from design to propose "Intelligent Design" as an alternative to the theory of evolution, and have provoked legal battles over what can and cannot be taught in public schools. But Intelligent Design still leaves questions about the intelligence of a design that leaves so many question marks, and the "evidence" produced by Intelligent Design leaves some asking why the Designer wasn't intelligent enough to produce a creation without the fingerprints of the Creator still visible.

3. Being and Reality

One of the most complicated arguments for the existence of God begins from the fact of existence and reasons that if there is reality, there must be an ultimate reality and that this ultimate reality is God. We will discuss this further in chapter 3, when we talk directly about God.

4. Love

In a similar way, some have suggested that the existence of love implies the existence of God. How, after all, could cold, impersonal forces produce a warm and personal result? Nothing, of course, is impossible, but it would be surprising if love could emerge out of the cold collision of atoms. Two people in love often feel that they have come into relationship not only with another person but with a force greater than themselves.

Such a line of reasoning seems more consistent with believing in a loving God than the arguments from cause or design. In those cases, the God who is proved to exist may, as we said, be a distant or even evil God, but the existence of a love beyond ourselves could hardly come from that sort of God. If love is really a power beyond ourselves, that power, by definition, is a loving power.

5. Reason and Doubt

When we talk about believing, we need to recognize that there are different kinds of reason or, better, that reason covers a wider spectrum of thought and experience than we usually recognize. It has been suggested that we have let the success of science in one area persuade us that only scientists use reason, whereas in fact we reason in many ways about many things. We use our human ability to reason when we invest in the stock market or plan a family vacation or choose one job over another. It is surely reasonable to marry someone when we fall in love; we may be very emotional about our decision, but most young couples do proceed in a logical way when they decide to marry and choose a place to live, and as they decide how responsibilities will be shared. Such decisions are not made scientifically; we don't usually test one potential spouse against another. But we do use our minds rationally to decide on a course of action that is reasonable. Scientists are beginning to look at the relationship between reason and emotion and to talk about "emotional intelligence." Perhaps we have made too sharp a separation between emotions and reason and should think more about the ways in which emotions guide and intensify reason, and reason guides and clarifies emotions.

While doubt is sometimes looked at as a weakness, it is also important to point out that doubt is an essential ingredient of a reasonable faith. Only when we doubt and question are we motivated to look for better answers. If we are to be believers, we need to keep the faculty of doubt active in our lives so as to encourage us to grow constantly into deeper and more mature faith. The nineteenth-century English poet Alfred Lord Tennyson said, "There lives more faith in honest doubt, believe me, than in half the creeds." Christianity at its best encourages questions, confident that good questions lead to deeper faith.

BELIEVING GROWS

One final note: believing is not an all-or-nothing proposition. It grows in us over time. This should be true of anything we do. If we run a small business, we hope to get better at it over time. If we become teachers, we should become more skillful at it with experience. If we are married, we ought to grow in love and understanding of the other. Life involves growth. Believing is not usually any different. We believe more deeply as time goes on. But growth in faith is not a simple steady development. It can stall for a time or even seem to run backwards. As the growth of a tree's roots may be invisible but vitally important, or as the human body grows even while sleeping, faith may be growing even when it seems absent from our lives. The questions that seem to overwhelm us at times may have value in deepening our understanding.

Some people have a radical conversion and seem to go from unbelief to belief at a single moment of decision. That radical change, however, may be the result of deep and invisible changes that we were unaware of until they broke through to our conscious awareness in a moment of time. Even so, our understanding of God still needs to continue to grow from that beginning, and over time come to a deeper and more mature faith.

Some people grow up as church members, but still must come to a time when the faith of their fathers and mothers becomes their own—and continues to grow. It has been said that "God has no grandchildren." We cannot simply inherit faith from our parents, but must come to a point when we know that faith to be our own.

We all experience faith in God in our own way. For some, faith is experienced primarily through the emotions and must be deeply authentic and convincing. For others, faith is more focused on the intellect, without a strongly emotional type of believing. Since believing is about your own individual relationship with God, it will probably be like your other relationships, depending on the kind of person you are. Your faith is your own and need not be like someone else's. Relax and grow into the kind of believer God has called you to be.

The 2 Bible

To talk about Christianity involves talking about the Bible sooner or later. Let's do it sooner.

Some Christians talk about the Bible as if it were an immutable fact of nature and a rock on which to build. They act as if they could say, "The Bible says..." and that would settle any matter or question that might arise. For others it's not that simple. Such people might ask, why should the Bible have any more authority for me than Shakespeare or the *New York Times*? There may be much wisdom within it, but it has to prove itself to me and I have every right to question it. No matter where each of us falls on the continuum of beliefs about the Bible, every Christian must at some point respond to the question of what authority the Bible has for me. What is it and why should I respect it?

WHAT IS THE BIBLE?

The Bible, to begin with, is not *a* book but a collection of books written and compiled over a span of a thousand years. These books include poetry and history and biography, laws and proverbs and visions; they are an unlikely accumulation of writings that seemed to unknown editors and collectors to sum up or embody the ways in which God has been made known to human beings.

Oddly enough for a volume of such importance to the church, there is not, in fact, one generally recognized collection of books that all Christians agree to call the Bible. There are sixty-six books recognized by almost all Christians, but Roman Catholics have longer versions of some books and a few additional books, the Eastern Orthodox churches recognize a slightly different collection, and Episcopalians put most of these additional books in a separate collection between the Old and New Testaments that they call the Apocrypha. Yet there is, as we said, general agreement on the authority of the sixty-six books which are most commonly offered in bookstores as a single volume called "the Bible."

The Hebrew Scriptures, aka the Old Testament

The "basic Bible," if we can call it that, begins with thirty-nine books that Christians inherited from Judaism. Jews today recognize as scripture a similar collection that they divide into three components. There is, first of all, the Law: the first five books of the Bible, which were once thought to have been written by Moses. These books, called the Pentateuch or Torah, tell the story of the creation of the world and the beginnings of the Jewish people, including the story of how God gave Moses the Ten Commandments at Mount Sinai and the development of that basic law into a complex code of behavior and worship. Second, there are the books of the Prophets, inspired men who spoke to the Hebrew people at various times in their history condemning their failures and calling them back to more faithful behavior. And finally there are the Writings, an eclectic collection of literature that includes proverbs and poetry and the great story of Job that wrestles with the problem of evil and why a good God would allow suffering. All these books were known and valued in Jesus' time and were accepted by the early church as the background and foundation on which they had been built.

They called them "the Old Testament," but increasingly Christians today call them "the Hebrew Scriptures."

The Christian Scriptures, aka the New Testament
The second and much smaller part of the Bible is the Christian Scriptures, commonly called "the New Testament." These twenty-seven books include four gospels that tell the story of the life and death and resurrection of Jesus; one history of the early church called the Acts of the Apostles; twenty-one letters written by Paul and other early Christian leaders; and the Book of Revelation, a vision of the end of the world and the worship in heaven that neatly balances the Book of Genesis where it all began.

THE AUTHORITY OF THE BIBLE

What gives this collection of books the authority it has? All Christians give the Bible a special place in their life and worship. Most would say it has "authority," but that would have a different meaning for members of various churches. For some, that "authority" is the final say on every aspect of life and worship; for others the Bible is the most important guideline but is subject to being balanced by Christian tradition and human reason; and still others would simply give the Bible great value while feeling free to question and reinterpret what it says.

There have been councils at various times in history that have agreed to accept these books as authoritative, but these councils could hardly impose their will on people unwilling to accept it. Another council might bring together the works of Shakespeare and Voltaire and Abraham Lincoln and declare them of equal or greater importance—but it would make no practical difference. We would almost certainly continue to study and respect or ignore them as before. So, too, with the books of the Bible. A council cannot *give* them authority, but it can *recognize* their authority. People over the centuries collected these books and read them and handed them on because the books had a unique character: they conveyed a wisdom and a knowledge of God that gave them weight and value in guiding human lives and helping them understand and respond to God. The Bible comes to us with the authority of that experience. The Bible has authority because so many millions have valued it over long periods of time and in many different cultures, and we respect the accumulated wisdom of that experience. Even so, individuals will have to discover that authority for themselves by reading the Bible and reflecting on it and deciding whether it helps them to understand the meaning and purpose of life. If it does, they will probably continue to turn to it for guidance and continue to deepen their understanding of the message it contains.

The truth of the Bible

Much more important than the differences among Christian churches over what books to include in the Bible are the differences among Christians as to what the Bible means and how it should be read. There are frequent stories in the news about these differences and the divisions they create. The word that sums up the problem is "fundamentalism," a word that summarizes an attitude toward understanding the Bible that sees every word as the literal word of God and therefore not to be questioned. While many other Christians affirm the Bible as the word of God, at the same time they believe we are free to interpret it in various ways, and it is in the area of interpretation that the differences and divisions arise.

The problem is most obvious when we read the first chapter of the first book of the Bible and find a story about the creation of the world. If the story is "literally" true, God created the world in six days, making the earth first and then adding the sun and moon and stars. This obviously contradicts everything science tells us about the origins of the universe. Later we come to the story of a great flood that destroyed all life on earth except for a man called Noah, who built an ark and saved his own family and two each of all the animals. Geologists have found no evidence of such a flood and nonfundamentalist literalists find it hard to imagine that an ark of the size described in the Bible (roughly half again the length of a football field and half as wide and four stories high) could have held two each of every form of animal life. How, they wonder, could Noah have fed them for the six months the flood lasted, especially since some of the animals would have needed to eat others of them?

Fundamentalists do not worry about such questions since in their view God obviously would have been able to do whatever was needed to make it work. But other Christians see no reason to disregard science and find it more helpful to understand the first eleven chapters of the Bible as "myth," stories containing important truths but not to be taken as historically true. We read Shakespeare and other great literature in a similar way. Whether Hamlet and King Lear ever existed is really irrelevant; the plays in which we find them contain great wisdom and we learn more every time we read them. So, too, with the story of creation and the stories of Adam and Eve and the Flood and the Tower of Babel. They are true in a deeper sense than mere historical fact. God did create the world. The first human beings, like all human beings, did lie to each other and do things they knew to be wrong, and the evil in human hearts cannot be washed away by a flood. To argue over whether these stories are literally true seems to be missing the point.

Here, as in our earlier discussion of believing, we encounter the basic question of how we decide what is true and what we believe. We cannot "prove" the truth of a story; we can only decide what is true to our experience and our understanding of the world. If these stories lead us to such a deeper understanding, then they are true for us in the only way that matters. They will guide and strengthen us as we live out our lives on earth and lead us into a deeper relationship with our Creator. Of course, the fact that the Bible has spoken so deeply to so many will add weight to the truth we find and persuade us to continue to seek meaning and value even when a first reading seems difficult to understand.

THE STORY OF THE BIBLE

Once we read past the first eleven chapters of Genesis, we find ourselves following the story of Abraham and his descendants, which is common ground to some degree for Jews and Christians and Muslims. The members of the three great "Abrahamic faiths," in spite of real and deep differences, remain "People of the Book"—descendants of Abraham and worshipers of one God.

With the story of Abraham we enter the arena of human history, dealing with real people who lived in real places. These stories were handed on by word of mouth for centuries before people had become literate and could write them down, and therefore we find duplications and exaggerations and even errors of fact in the stories, but the essential narrative shows us what we need to know. We can follow the story of real people as they acquired a basic knowledge of God and learned what it means to live in a conscious relationship with that God.

The story of Israel

As we follow the story of Abraham's descendants, the family grows and becomes a group of tribes and these tribes become slaves in Egypt. The second book of the Bible, Exodus, tells the story of their escape from Egypt and their encounter with

God at the volcano of Sinai through which they acquire the Ten Commandments or Decalogue, the fundamental laws by which they are to regulate their life. The remaining three books of the Pentateuch—Leviticus, Numbers, and Deuteronomy—spell out the laws the Hebrews developed to regulate their community life and the details of their worship. Most Christians find all this largely irrelevant to their lives today and their eyes tend to glaze over as they wander deeper and deeper into the minute details of these laws, but there are passages in these books that shine like gold when we stumble on them. In the Book of Leviticus, for example, we find the command that Christians often, wrongly, imagine came from Jesus: "You shall love your neighbor as yourself."

In these passages from the law we come again to the problem of how the Bible speaks to us. When we find directions for the treatment of leprosy or a prohibition of using two kinds of thread in the same cloth, are we required to follow these instructions literally? When we read that it is an abomination for a man to lie with a man as with a woman, are we to abominate homosexual behavior and, if so, continue to read the second half of the verse commanding that such people be stoned to death? And should adulterers also be put to death, as required in the verses immediately before? What does it mean to be "People of the Book"? We constantly encounter the same problem in various ways: can we choose to listen to the passages that please us and ignore the rest? Thomas Jefferson famously went through the Bible with scissors and paste and constructed a Bible to his own liking. Following that procedure, a congregation with a hundred members might construct a hundred different Bibles to be read on Sunday morning.

How, then, can Christians claim to respect the authority of a book that poses enormous obstacles for some and is read with different understandings by almost everyone? What is the "authority" that gives the Bible such wide appeal in spite of the problems?

Truth in poetry and story
The answer to this question may begin with a broader survey of the component books of the Bible and, perhaps, with the book you will find if you open your Bible in the middle. The Book of Psalms gives us what may be the most familiar passage of the Bible, Psalm 23, which begins, "The LORD is my shepherd, I shall not want. "

Consider the statements we find in this ancient poem: "I shall not want. He makes me lie down in green pastures.... Your rod and your staff—they comfort me." None of this, surely, is to be taken literally, but the picture it conjures up is translated automatically by our minds into terms that speak to us. We are reassured and strengthened and comforted in our various situations by this imagery even though we may never have met a real shepherd or been made to lie down in a green pasture.

Think then of the stories Jesus told. We call them parables, and some of these stories are so well known they have become part of our language. So many people know the parable of the Good Samaritan, for example, that the title is commonly used to speak of situations where people went out of their way to help others. We say, "He was truly a Good Samaritan," although we may have no idea what Samaritans are. In the same way, we may speak of a "prodigal son" or a "lost sheep." The stories Jesus told were not literally true, but they convey a timeless message that is very easy to hear and understand. In all these situations, the "literal truth" of the Bible is not determined by its conformity to historical fact. "Poetic truth," as we might call it, is a deeper kind of truth and more important.

The "truth" of the story of Noah or the story of Adam and Eve is only slightly different. These stories are also true in teaching us something of the way God deals with the world. It has been called "relational truth" because it clarifies our relationship with God. On the other hand, even though the story of David and Bathsheba was almost certainly historically true, its importance for us is not much different from the importance of the story of Noah: it teaches relational truth by showing us how David sinned and how he repented. Biblical truth, then, need not be a matter of verifiable fact in many cases. We value many of the stories because of what we learn from them that applies to us, quite apart from their literal truth.

Truth in human history
Red flags, however, must be raised at this point. No doubt some Christians—many, perhaps, without really thinking about it—take the whole Bible in this poetic sense and never trouble themselves about the truth or historical reality of any of it. Yet this way of interpreting the Bible can lead to unfortunate misunderstandings. Christianity, like Judaism, is a religion based on an historical record of what God has done in the world. It is not an imaginary world or a purely rational philosophy, but a knowledge of God based on historical events. Real people escaped from real slavery in Egypt and were really carried into exile in Babylon. A real person named Jesus was born in Palestine some two thousand years ago. He called disciples, healed and taught, "suffered under Pontius Pilate, was crucified, died, and was buried," and rose again to life. "These things," Paul once said, "were not done in a corner."

These historical foundations of Christianity have a profound connection to Christian believing and theology. Some Christians over the centuries, for example, have denied the physical resurrection of Jesus and instead have suggested that to speak of Jesus' resurrection is to speak poetically; for them, the resurrection is really just a way of talking about his continuing influence. We will come back to this subject later. What matters here is simply to point out that while there is poetry and poetic speech in the Bible, there is also an historical record of specific events from which Christians have come to understand more fully who God is and what God's purpose is for us.

The expectation of a messiah

Because the Hebrews believed that God had acted in their history they had expectations that ran far ahead of their actual experience. God had rescued them from slavery, led them into the promised land, and given them greatness under David and Solomon. But then it all came apart. Solomon's successors divided the kingdom and the two smaller kingdoms were defeated in war. The smaller, northern kingdom of Israel disappeared from history and the leaders of the larger, southern kingdom of Judah were carried into exile. Had the promises of God, then, failed? That would have been a reasonable guess, except that the prophets continued to speak of God's promise and raise that expectation higher still. The prophet Isaiah envisioned a "peaceable kingdom" in which the lion and lamb will dwell together and "a little child will lead them."

How exactly this would happen was left unclear. Some speculated that God would send an angel, others expected a second David, others that God would intervene directly in human history to establish a "messianic" kingdom. The "messiah," or anointed one (*Christ* is the Greek word) would come and save the people from defeat and failure. Perhaps the messiah would conquer other kingdoms. Perhaps all nations would be drawn to Jerusalem in worship.

These expectations began apparently while the Jews were in exile in Babylon. They provided hope when it would have been natural to despair. When the exile ended and the Jews were able to return to Palestine, it seemed at first that the messianic hopes were being fulfilled. But the restored kingdom was not nearly as great as the kingdom of David and Solomon. Once again, hope was kept alive by a messianic expectation that was raised higher in the midst of despair.

Instead of a new kingdom of David, the Jews found themselves absorbed into the Greek Empire that dominated the Middle East for well over a century. Some of that story is found in the books of the Maccabees in the Apocrypha. Then the Greeks were defeated by the Romans and the Jewish people were subjugated to Rome. As the grip of the Roman Empire tightened, hope of a messiah rose higher still and more than once a leader proclaimed himself the promised one only to be defeated and killed. At last the Jews rebelled against Roman rule so effectively that it required a major effort on the part of Rome to put down the revolt and reassert their rule. Jerusalem was destroyed in the process and Jews were scattered abroad throughout the Roman Empire. That rebellion took place in 70 CE, less than forty years after the lifetime of Jesus of Nazareth.

Stories about Jesus

It was in this time of Roman rule that a man called Jesus called a little group of followers together and taught them a different way of being Jewish. He claimed to respect the Law of Moses, but he taught that the law was given to enhance human freedom, not to enslave us. If an animal was suffering because it had fallen into a hole, it was more important to pull it out than to follow the literal interpretation of the law not to work on the Sabbath day. Jesus believed people who were ill should be healed even on the Sabbath, and the hungry should be able to eat even the holy bread on the altar if necessary. Tithing and fasting were all very well, but humility and love for others were what mattered most. All this shocked and threatened the authorities and may have been the primary reason they conspired to have Jesus killed.

It seems likely that Jesus' active ministry of teaching lasted only three years, but stories about him continued to circulate after his death and resurrection and within a generation they began to be written down. The records about Jesus that have come down to us are based on these widely circulated stories. The earliest is the one called the Gospel according to Mark, and it is obvious in looking at it that it is really a collection of short stories: the author has pieced together a story about how someone was healed, a story about how Jesus called the first disciples or followers, a story about how Jesus responded when his teaching was questioned by the authorities, and so on. The longest story, over a third of the gospel, is the story of the last week of Jesus' life: how he was welcomed to Jerusalem as the promised messiah, how the authorities plotted against him, how he was crucified, and how his tomb was found empty on the third day.

This first gospel was used as the basis for two longer versions of the story called the Gospel according to Matthew and the Gospel according to Luke. These versions of the story reshape Mark's narrative in different ways. Matthew's gospel seems to be focused on a community with a dominant Jewish element and points again and again to the way the life and ministry of Jesus fulfilled the expectations of the Jews. Matthew's gospel even divides Jesus' teaching into five blocks of material, as if to parallel the first five books of the Bible, which are known as the Torah and are at the heart of the Hebrew Scriptures. The best known of these blocks of teaching is the so-called Sermon on the Mount, which begins with the series of blessings known as the Beatitudes and includes the Golden Rule.

Luke's version of Jesus' story is written in the most polished Greek and tells us more than the other gospel accounts about Jesus' mother, Mary, and about the women who followed Jesus. It also emphasizes more strongly Jesus' concern for the poor and disadvantaged, and tells us the best known of Jesus' parables—the stories of the Prodigal Son and the Good Samaritan.

The Gospel according to John, the fourth gospel, takes a very different approach. The first three gospels (sometimes called the synoptic gospels, because they see with "one eye") tell us about Jesus' ministry in northern Palestine, the region around the Sea of Galilee, and only mention one visit to Jerusalem, at the end of Jesus' life. John's gospel, on the other hand, tells of three visits to Jerusalem. John gives us no parables, but there are long passages describing conversations with his disciples in which Jesus calls himself "the light of the world" and "the bread of life" and "the true vine." While there is no mention of bread and wine in John's account of the Last Supper, he quotes Jesus earlier as saying that those who eat his flesh and drink his blood will live forever. In these and other metaphors and images found in John's gospel we see a Jesus who is much more direct about who he is. Indeed, John's gospel begins by telling us that "in the beginning was the Word" and that this "Word became flesh and lived among us." In other words, Jesus is God's eternal Word. Yet John also speaks of Jesus as becoming tired and thirsty and weeping at the grave of a friend in a very human way. John confronts us with the puzzle that the first Christians wrestled with (and we still do!): Who is Jesus, and how is he related to God? This is the central question for anyone exploring Christian faith.

The early church

After the gospels we come to a book that tells us about the early days of the church. Called the Acts of the Apostles, it was written by the author of Luke's gospel as a sequel and carries the narrative that began in Galilee and ended in Jerusalem, from Jerusalem onward to Rome. Like the gospels, Acts is a compilation of stories from several sources. There are stories of the first days of the church in Jerusalem and stories of Paul's missionary journeys and, finally, a section that reads like a travel diary that might have been kept by Luke as he traveled to Rome with Paul. Like so much of the Old Testament, this too is history and shows us God at work in human affairs.

Letters to young churches

The next twenty-one books of the New Testament are letters written by various authors to churches and individuals that give us a different way of looking at the early church's life. They show us individuals and congregations attempting to understand what it meant to be a Christian. Should they carry on Jewish traditions? Should they separate themselves from their pagan neighbors? Should they think in terms of Jesus coming again soon or in terms of a long future? Perhaps a third of these letters were written by Paul himself; others were written by people who were influenced by Paul. Some of the letters seem to be from other local communities of Christians and from very different viewpoints. Thus in these early letters we have varying perspectives on how the first Christians thought about their lives and mission, and they aren't always quite consistent. Nor do they necessarily apply directly to the twenty-first-century church.

A vision of heaven

The last book of the Bible is called the Revelation to John
and consists of a series of visions of the end of the world and
of worship in heaven. The book was written in a time of persecution and the ultimate message of the author is, "Hold
on; help is on the way. God will reward those who are faithful and destroy those who persecute you." The author bor-
rows a good deal of his language from the Book of Daniel,
which was written in a similar time of persecution under the
Greek Empire.

What relevance does language borrowed from a pre-
Christian Jewish source to strengthen first-century Christians persecuted by Rome have for Christians in
twenty-first-century America? Some try to translate it by
equating Rome with Washington, while others see the imagery as a coded picture of international affairs, especially in
the Middle East. The great majority of biblical scholars
would probably agree that Revelation is not a picture in code
of the twenty-first-century world and that we only create
problems for ourselves by attempting to apply it in that way.

There can be no doubt, however, that certain passages
provide great comfort at times of loss and bereavement:

> They will hunger no more, and thirst no more;
>> the sun will not strike them,
>> nor any scorching heat;
> for the Lamb at the center of the throne
>> will be their shepherd,
>> and he will guide them to springs of the
>>> water of life,
> and God will wipe away every tear from their eyes.
>
> (Revelation 7:16–17)

It would be impossible to draw a literal picture of a "Lamb
at the center of the throne" and God wiping away "every

tear" from our eyes, but as with so many of the passages in
the Bible, no translation is necessary. We know what it
means and can apply it to our lives.

SUMMARY
Although Christians vary widely in their ways of reading and
understanding the Bible, it remains the basic document of
Christian faith and will always repay further prayerful study.
Because it comes from so many different circumstances over
a long span of time, some parts will commend themselves to
us more than others, but, like a complex tapestry, each section, however obscure at first, can contribute something to
an understanding of the whole.

Most important, perhaps, is the fact that these books
come to us from a long span of time and a wide variety of
human circumstances. Their societies were very different
from ours, but as we see them struggling to understand what
God was doing in their world and what they were called to
do in response, we can find guidance in our own struggles.
God's people are called to live in faith and patience and, always, with love for others. They are called to make a difference in their society or, in Jesus' own example, to be like the
leaven that transforms the lump of dough into bread which
is the staff of life.

God

Several years ago, a book was published that tried to show how God had evolved from a savage and primitive deity in the early books of the Old Testament into the more sophisticated and merciful New Testament God. Perhaps this understanding of the God of the Bible is one way of looking at it, but it seems likelier that it is actually human society that has changed. Other cynics have said that humankind created God in its own image, and there is some truth to that. We have great difficulty understanding anyone unlike us, so of course we speak of God in human terms. What else could we do?

The first thing to understand in thinking about God is that any picture of God we produce will be limited by our human self-centeredness. The childhood notion of God as an old man with a long beard on a cloud may evolve into something much less literally humanoid, but we still remain limited by our brains and our language system. Our words were created to define the things we know and when we try to use them to talk about God they can't help sounding a lot like us.

The usual way we try to avoid this problem is by using words that are not taken so directly from human life. We speak about a "Force," as in *Star Wars,* or a "Power Beyond

Ourselves." The trouble with that approach is that it diminishes God to something less than ourselves, rather than more. A volcano or hurricane has force and a power beyond ourselves, but we would not be likely to speak of it as loving or merciful. Those are human characteristics, and a God who is loving and merciful is like us—at our best—in that respect. There is nothing wrong with using the only words we have to talk about God, as long as we remember that they will not be adequate.

A key word for a Christian definition of God is "personal." We will have to spend a good deal of time thinking about what that means, but it establishes a bottom line: God is like us, only more so. God is more than we are, not less. A God who is simply a force would be impersonal and therefore less than we are. A God who is personal is a God who is like us at our best—only more so.

The God of the Bible is first of all a personal God. God looks for Adam and Eve in the Garden of Eden in the cool of the day and stops to talk with Abraham outside his tent. Much is left to the imagination in these stories, but the important point is that the God of the Bible is a God who enters into personal relationships with human beings. As the biblical story moves on, the picture of God expands and words become less able to describe God. God appears to Moses in a burning bush and, later, comes to him on Mount Sinai in cloud and thunder. Still later, when God appeared to the prophet Elijah, there was "a great wind, so strong that it was splitting mountains and breaking rocks in pieces before the LORD, but the LORD was not in the wind; and after the wind an earthquake, but the LORD was not in the earthquake; and after the earthquake a fire, but the LORD was not in the fire; and after the fire a sound of sheer silence" (1 Kings 19:11–12). In other words, God is beyond any "force" we can imagine and silence speaks louder than words.

HOW DO WE TALK ABOUT GOD?

How, then, can we talk about God when words fail us? There are several answers to this question, and we use them frequently in ordinary life.

The negative way

First of all, when words fail us, we tend to say, "It's not like that." When we don't have the words to convey adequately what we are trying to describe, we often resort to words that describe what we *don't* mean. God is not an old man with a beard. God does not live on Mount Olympus. A large part of the Bible is devoted to ruling out false understandings of God: God does not tolerate injustice; God is not in the storm and whirlwind; God does not abandon God's people.

When Christians set out to explain their faith in the early centuries of the church, they often got it wrong and had terrible arguments about who Jesus was. Often they had to settle for negative solutions: Jesus was not merely human; Jesus was not merely divine. A lot of scientific research goes through a similar process: this drug does not cure cancer; this therapy is not effective for backache. We rule out the answers that do not work and see what we have left. In fact, a lot of the words we use about God are really negative words. "Almighty" and "omniscient" are not precise definitions; they simply tell us God is not limited in power or knowledge. But what unlimited power and knowledge might be like, we have no idea. It is not part of our common human experience. To use such words is not only to say that God is beyond our understanding, but also to say that there is *something* or *someone* there, although we have no words that are adequate to describe who or what it is.

A diagram of the Trinity that is often used to explain this concept has a central circle labeled "God" and three circles in a triangle around the central circle labeled "Father," "Son," and "Holy Spirit." Lines are then drawn connecting each circle in the triangle to the center, and along each line is the word "IS." So the Father IS God, the Son IS God, and the Holy Spirit IS God. Other lines are drawn connecting the circles in the triangle and along each of those lines are the word "IS NOT." So the Father IS NOT the Son and the Son IS NOT the Father, and the Holy Spirit IS NOT the Father or the Son. The negative statements are just as important as the positive statements in clarifying our understanding of God.

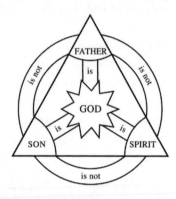

It is interesting to notice that the church has usually issued statements about who God is or is not only in response to false statements. It is easier to rule out false statements than to construct true statements that will be completely satisfactory.

Along with the commonly used Apostles' Creed and Nicene Creed, there is a third creed that has come down to us from the early days of the Christian church called the Athanasian Creed. Much of what it asserts is in negative form: "The Father [is] not created, the Son [is] not created, the Holy Spirit [is] not created. The Father incomprehensible, the Son incomprehensible, and the Holy Spirit incomprehensible. . . . Yet there are not three incomprehensibles, nor three uncreated."

One early Christian called Dionysius spelled it out even further in his treatise on "The Mystical Theology," in which he maintains that God "is not soul, or mind, or endowed with the faculty of imagination, conjecture, reason, or understanding; nor is it any act of reason or understanding; nor

can it be described by the reason or perceived by the understanding, since it is not number, or order, or greatness, or
littleness, or equality, or inequality, and since it is not im-
movable nor in motion, or at rest, and is not power or light,"
for any description of God, positive or negative, transcends
all human words and is "free from every limitation and beyond them all."

Some may feel that one incomprehensible is more than
enough and that not much is clarified by all these negations.
Yes, but it makes one thing very clear: at the heart of God is
a mystery beyond human understanding.

Analogies

A second and more positive way that Christians can use language about God is through the use of analogies. We use
analogies every day when we say one thing is like another. If
you have never been to Scotland, I might tell you it is like
Colorado. If you have never seen a tangerine, I could say it
is like an orange with a loose skin. When we speak of God
as "Father," we are making an analogy, saying that God is
like a human father in caring and providing for a family. God
is also like a shepherd and a rock and a fire. One basic word
the Bible uses for God is "merciful," and that word in Hebrew comes from the word for the womb. God is therefore
like a mother who cares for the child of her womb.

When we read the New Testament, we find Jesus using
analogies again and again. He said that the kingdom of
heaven is like a pearl and a seed and a net full of fish and a
king who invited guests to a feast. The kingdom of heaven
is not literally a pearl or a seed or a feast, but it is like each
of them in important ways, and these analogies help us to
understand better what the kingdom of God is like.

However, it is important to be careful with analogies.
When we say God is like a Father, we are not saying that

God IS a Father. Dionysius would have been quick to point
out that God is also NOT a Father. Those aspects of human
fatherhood that are most loving and caring give us a glimpse
of what God is like, but God is not like the father who gets
drunk on weekends or forgets a birthday or anniversary. God
is also like a mother—and also NOT like a mother. These
are analogies and they have only limited value. The minute
we forget that, we forget the mystery and limit God to our
human understanding.

Nouns and adjectives

Adjectives can also help us. We use any number of them to
speak of God: good, just, powerful, merciful, wise, patient,
and so on. But adjectives also can be misleading. Children
may not study English grammar anymore, but when they
did, they learned that adjectives modify nouns. A "good
man" is a man who does good things. A "red hat" is a hat of
a red color.

What they do not teach in school is that nouns also modify adjectives. "Good" is a useful adjective, but it means different things in different contexts. A "good dog" is one that
will roll over on command and fetch a stick. A "good child,"
on the other hand, is not expected to roll over on command
and fetch sticks but rather to get homework done on time
and to respect his or her parents. When I say I have a "good
computer," "good" means something very different from
what it means when I speak about a "good tomato."

When we speak about God, that noun modifies any adjective we use. Goodness in God is different from goodness
in dogs or human beings. We cannot fully understand God's
goodness. Sometimes it seems to us that God's goodness is
not good at all. We need to understand that when we apply
the adjective "good" to God, it is being bent so far out of
shape that it is almost unrecognizable. Some might want to

say, "If God doesn't act the way I would act, God is not good." But that would be measuring God by human standards; it would be like saying that the child who doesn't fetch sticks is not a good child. Nevertheless, we have to use the only words we have, and even in their limitations they give us some kind of clue to the nature of God. They point us in the right direction, although they can never get us all the way there.

The way of paradox

Another way to speak of God is the way of paradox. A paradox is something that seems to contradict itself and yet is true. Modern science provides a number of paradoxes, such as the statement that an electron is both a wave and a particle or that if we know the speed of an electron we cannot know its location and vice versa. The Bible is full of paradoxes: it speaks of Jesus as both judge and advocate, as the Lion of Judah and the Lamb that was slain. God is called the Alpha and the Omega, the beginning and the end. Dionysius, in the way of negation, said that God is neither affirmation nor negation. Several centuries later the Franciscan scholar Bonaventure said, "God is a circle whose center is everywhere and whose circumference is nowhere." St. Paul described himself to the church in Corinth as "poor, yet making many rich; as having nothing, and yet possessing everything." The ultimate Christian paradox is the affirmation that Jesus is truly human and truly God.

Here, again, we face the limits of human words and are forced to use language in a way that seems contradictory, and yet points toward a truth beyond our experience.

The way of imagery

Still one more way to speak of God is through the use of images. The Bible says that human beings are made in the

image of God. That leaves us free to wonder how we are like
God. Is it because we are creative or because we use language
or because we are capable of love? All of this is true within
limits and enables us to say that human beings reveal something of God. So, also, a city can reveal God both negatively
and positively—which is a paradox. We can look at the worst
aspects of a city, the dirt and crime, and say, "Heaven is not
like that." Yet in the Book of Revelation, Jerusalem becomes
an image of heaven. A city has the potential to reflect God's
ultimate purpose for humanity. Even New York City, for all
its flaws, reflects human creativity—all the best art and music
and architecture—and a community in which all the races
of humanity work together, however imperfectly, in a way
that shows us something of human potential.

So language enables us to say God is like this and not like
that, and can be revealed in the images and analogies we recognize, and thus we come to some better understanding of
who God is. Keeping all that in mind, we need to see more
specifically what the Bible says about God.

THE BIBLICAL PICTURE OF GOD
God is a God of power

We have already said that the Bible portrays God as personal,
as loving and caring. But the earliest images of God recorded
in the Bible are much simpler. They come not from the stories in the first chapters of Genesis, in fact, but rather from
some of the psalms. Poetry is more easily remembered than
prose, and some of the psalms seem to come from a much
earlier time and to reflect an idea of God coming from the
Hebrew experience of the volcano at Mount Sinai and their
years spent wandering in the desert. Psalm 18 provides one
example of this early understanding of God as a God of
earthquake and storm:

Then the earth reeled and rocked;
    the foundations also of the mountains trembled
    and quaked, because he was angry.
Smoke went up from his nostrils,
    and devouring fire from his mouth;
    glowing coals flamed forth from him.
He bowed the heavens, and came down;
    thick darkness was under his feet.
He rode on a cherub, and flew;
    he came swiftly upon the wings of the wind.
He made darkness his covering around him,
    his canopy thick clouds dark with water.
Out of the brightness before him
    there broke through his clouds
    hailstones and coals of fire.
The LORD also thundered in the heavens,
    and the Most High uttered his voice.

(Psalm 18:7–13)

Now, God is not a volcano or a storm, but volcano and storm are, like God, a power beyond human power. They provide a good place to begin in our understanding of God. However much else we may learn about God, it remains true that God's power is infinitely far beyond our own. Human beings have always tried to control God for their own ends. We try to bargain with God: "I will offer sacrifices in your temple, if you will give me a good harvest"; "I will reform my habits, if you will give me a better job"; "I will say my prayers every day, if you will cure my cancer." But a God who is first known as a God of terrifying power is one with whom bargains cannot be made. We can hide from such power or we can try to serve it. The Hebrews, at their best, learned to serve the God they had encountered. They moved beyond their instinctive fear to worship and obey.

God is a God of justice

When the Hebrew people arrived at Mount Sinai in their escape from Egypt, they were given a terrifying display of power. The mountain quaked and they trembled. But it was also at Mount Sinai that they were given the Ten Commandments and became a people whose lives were guided by law. Law is useful: it provides guidance out of past experience as to how God would have us live. But law is fundamentally negative: while it tells us what we cannot do, it is less useful in guiding us in a positive direction.

It is also true that human beings often become self-righteous when they feel that they have kept the law and earned God's approval. The Pharisees of Jesus' time tried harder to please God than any people had ever done, and succeeded only in earning a reputation as narrow-minded, self-righteous legalists. Christians have often fallen into the same trap. We want to please God and we want simple rules that will enable us to do that. So churches and Christian teachers provide rules for Christian behavior: go to church every week, read the Bible, say your prayers, give up fish on Friday and dessert in Lent, don't play cards, don't go dancing, don't smoke or drink, and so on. Some of these may be very good habits to form, but in themselves they will not make us more like God. Laws are good, but they cannot by themselves create a just society. On the contrary, rules can be merely oppressive. Justice is much more than obeying the law.

When Elijah met with God, he passed through the earthquake, wind, and fire and heard "a sound of sheer silence." Elijah and the prophets began to show the Hebrew people a God who was more than a God of power. Amos is the prophet who expressed it best when he spoke of God as a God of justice. God had rescued the Hebrews from slavery with the power that swept back the Red Sea and destroyed Pharaoh's army. That was not simply power but power with a purpose, and the purpose was not simply to rescue the Hebrew people but to establish justice. The Jews had been enslaved and God's power set them free because slavery is against God's will. By the time of Amos, centuries later, they had gained enough power to enslave others. Therefore, Amos prophesied, they would be destroyed as surely as Pharaoh's army. A just God plays no favorites. You cannot bargain with God, Amos said:

> Even though you offer me your burnt offerings
> and grain offerings, I will not accept them;
> and the offerings of well-being of your fatted
> animals I will not look upon.
> Take away from me the noise of your songs;
> I will not listen to the melody of your harps.
> But let justice roll down like waters,
> and righteousness like an ever-flowing stream.
> (Amos 5:22–24)

God is merciful

Amos and the prophets were right. They saw that a nation relying on God's favor but not seeking to be like God would be defeated eventually. We cannot be like God in having power and not be like God in being just. So, indeed, the kingdom was destroyed and their leaders were carried into exile in Babylon. There they learned a third lesson: God is merciful.

In the time of exile, the prophets began to speak of forgiveness and mercy. God still had a purpose that the Jews could serve. God would restore them and bring them back to the promised land and let them build again. The Book of Isaiah contains familiar prophecies from that time:

> Comfort, O comfort my people,
> says your God.

Speak tenderly to Jerusalem,
    and cry to her that she has served her term,
    that her penalty is paid,
    that she has received from the LORD's hand
        double for all her sins. . . .
Say to the cities of Judah,
    "Here is your God!"
See, the Lord GOD comes with might,
    and his arm rules for him;
his reward is with him,
    and his recompense before him.
He will feed his flock like a shepherd;
he will gather the lambs in his arms,
    and carry them in his bosom,
    and gently lead the mother sheep.
                    (Isaiah 40:1–2, 9–11)

The messiah

After seventy years of exile, the Jews in Babylon were set free to return to Jerusalem and build again. But they could not regain the wealth and power they had had in earlier times. They had dreamed of a restored Israel as a place of peace and prosperity where God's law would be perfectly kept and they would "see their children's children, and peace upon Israel." It didn't happen, but the dreams persisted. After all, God had called them for a purpose and therefore the dreams were expanded and pushed further into the future. The dreams took a variety of forms. In some, God would send a second David to restore their fortunes. In some, they would know such peace that the natural order would be transformed and the lion would lie down with the lamb.

These hopes and dreams centered more and more on the idea of a messiah, an anointed one, a chosen servant of God who would come at last to fulfill God's purpose. They had come to understand that the personal God who had once spoken with Moses face to face could not be seen or confined to any image or representation, but God's purpose in history would at last be fulfilled in the person of a messianic savior.

In summary, the Old Testament picture of God developed over the centuries, as God's people came to see that God was at work in their history and was a God of power, justice, and mercy whose purpose had yet to be fulfilled. God could not be portrayed in the carved images of animals and the household gods that other people made, but God had become known as one who cared in a very personal way for the people God had created.

Jesus

Several years ago a leading theologian named Jaroslav Pelikan wrote a book called *Jesus Through the Centuries* in which he explored the various ways Jesus of Nazareth has been portrayed at different times. Jesus has been seen as the Prince of Peace at some times and as the Conqueror in others; he has been described as the wise teacher, stern judge, the Liberator, the Cosmic Christ, the Son of God, and the Son of Man. Theologians have struggled to balance a number of these different ways of seeing the first-century man Pelikan describes as "the dominant figure in the history of Western culture for almost twenty centuries." Certainly no one can talk intelligently about Western art or music or literature or political theory without some reference to Jesus. The cross has been a central image in Western art, just as the suffering and death of Jesus have been a constant theme in our music, while literary critics must always ask themselves whether a particular character is a "Christ figure" or not. Political theorists have responded to the gospel message of freedom on the one hand and the image of Jesus as king on the other. In one way or another, all these aspects of our culture—indeed, our culture itself—have been shaped by the followers of Jesus as they attempted to respond to his life and witness.

Inevitably, Christians and others have reexamined the original story again and again in an attempt to evaluate the various responses to the gospel about Jesus. At the turn of the twentieth century, scholars set out to rediscover "the historical Jesus," with mixed results. At the end of the century, scholars were still attempting to get behind the various images to discover some more solid basis for belief—or nonbelief. Is it possible at this late date to rediscover this dominant figure and understand who he is for us, what meaning his life has for twenty-first-century people?

We have already talked about the way in which the people of first-century Palestine had looked forward to a coming messiah who would fulfill their history, save them from the Romans, inaugurate a world kingdom, and so on. If we have trouble seeing Jesus as he was, so did they. We have trouble seeing Jesus through the varied portrayals of two thousand years, just as they had trouble seeing Jesus through the varied expectations of at least five centuries of their own religious experience. The challenge has been the same for Christians in every age. But perhaps the task is not so much to single out one picture of Jesus and discard the others as it is to give all of them their appropriate place. Each different picture is justified to some degree, or it would not have had wide appeal.

It is, then, an almost impossible task to tell in one short chapter who Jesus is and why he matters. Any analysis will be incomplete, satisfying perhaps to some but certainly inadequate to others. The task might be compared to asking a partner in marriage what her spouse means to her, or asking those who know them both why their relationship matters. People who know one or both of the partners will all have an opinion. Employer, employee, fellow worker, pastor, teacher, neighbor, parent, child: each will see some part of the faults and virtues of the partner they happen to know, but surely none of their accounts will seem adequate to the other partner—nor will that partner be able to set down the reasons for their love in a completely satisfying way. Moreover, their accounts of the relationship will change from one year to the next. Relationships evolve and grow, and what matters intensely early in a relationship may become almost irrelevant as time passes. A good relationship is sustained in many ways.

To give an account of the role of Jesus in Christian faith is not, then, a question of certain specific facts or definitions. Jesus is not a creedal statement to be affirmed line by line but a living person with whom Christians enter into a living and changing relationship. What matters in any useful account of the role of Jesus in Christianity is not so much a factual account or a theological analysis but some insight into the relationship between Jesus and the believer—a relationship that will seem somewhat different to every individual Christian and that will be constantly changing as time passes, as experience broadens, and as needs change. We can only attempt to tell the story as factually as possible, describe something of what that story has meant to various people at various times, and then suggest what it may mean—what Jesus may mean—to a Christian today. That, too, will differ depending on the age and ethnicity and social surrounding and personal relationships of each individual. But the problem is not so much defining Jesus as it is one of understanding ourselves. If Jesus is who Christians claim him to be, he cannot be confined to any one role or image. He is capable of being all things to all people; he is life and truth for all and it is because of our own limitations that we produce such varied and limited pictures of him.

To ask who Jesus is for us, we need to ask who we are and what our needs and expectations are, and to consider how these have been shaped by our upbringing and experience. If we are looking for a personal Savior, Jesus has been just that for many. If we are looking for healing or guidance or a perspective on social problems, all these are potentially present. But if we focus on one or another of these, we should remember that others will come with differing agendas which may be as valid as ours—or more so. We need, then, to remain open to new perspectives that may clash with ours and be as prepared to learn from others as we hope they will be to hear us. In all the hundreds and thousands of Christian groups determined to persuade others of their particular outlook not all can be right, but many of them may have insights from which we can learn. No one individual or church at any one period of time can possibly contain all truth. There is always more to learn. Christianity remains an adventure into ever fuller understanding of the ultimately unknowable God.

JESUS' LIFE AND MINISTRY

That a man called Jesus lived in the land now called Israel some two thousand years ago is as well attested as almost any fact of history. There are wonderful stories of his birth that are told again every year in late December and provide an excuse for celebration and gift-giving even in countries like Japan, where Christians are a tiny minority of the population. But two of the four gospels that tell the story of Jesus' life ignore these birth narratives entirely. For Mark and John the story begins with Jesus' baptism in the Jordan River at (probably) the age of thirty and his setting out on a brief ministry, during which he traveled never more than some fifty to seventy-five miles from the town where he grew up. It seems likely that this public ministry of Jesus lasted for only three years, from his baptism in the Jordan to his death by crucifixion in Jerusalem.

At the center of these three years of ministry was a small group of followers Jesus selected to be with him and learn from him. He taught them separately from his public sermons and sent them out on training missions, preparing them carefully to carry on his ministry. It seems, in other words, that he thought of himself as more than a wise man imparting wisdom to his immediate audience. A chosen few were being prepared to carry on his ministry after his death and resurrection.

So what was that ministry? The gospels tell of sick people being cured, of stories being told, and of a growing conflict between Jesus and the existing Jewish authorities. These stories are loosely strung together in a narrative that moves from its beginning in the northern part of Palestine around the Lake of Galilee toward a final climactic week in Jerusalem, where Jesus went with his disciples to celebrate the Passover, the Jewish freedom festival that commemorated their escape from slavery in Egypt many centuries earlier. In all four gospels a major part of the story is devoted to the last week in Jerusalem and the story of Jesus' crucifixion and resurrection.

Healing

That Jesus healed many people is beyond dispute. In Mark's gospel, the earliest account of Jesus' ministry, well over a quarter of his material (not counting the story of the last week in Jerusalem) concerns healings. There are several stories of people "possessed by evil spirits," two of paralysis, two of blind men, one of a deaf man, references to people cured of "various diseases," and one story of a girl apparently brought back to life. The later gospels, even Luke's which has the reputation of a special concern for healing, spend much less time telling of these healings, though they remain significant. In Matthew's gospel the emphasis is much more heavily on teaching, but still some 10 to 15 percent of his material, apart from stories of Jesus' birth and, again, of the last week, tells of healings.

Of course these healings, of themselves, prove very little. There were apparently others who also healed in Jesus' time, and there is abundant evidence that healings take place today as a result of faith. Roman Catholics and others still flock to Lourdes and similar shrines where healings occur. Evangelicals produce flamboyant preachers who heal many. And quieter ministries of healing take place week by week in churches that invite all who come to receive a laying on of hands for themselves or others. Clergy of several churches anoint the sick in hospitals, churches, and elsewhere. Those who have investigated the phenomenon speak of "psychosomatic" healings and say that the human body is not a mere machine that can be set right with the proper medicine or surgery but a complex unity of mind and body, some would say "soul and body." Sometimes human beings become ill— paralyzed, possessed, depressed, deaf, blind, crippled in many ways—for no purely physical reason and can be healed, released from the illness, without physical treatment. So Jesus undoubtedly healed but that fact is not significant by itself.

Miracles

In addition to stories of healing, there are stories of events outside the normal range of human experience. There are stories of Jesus walking on water, calming a storm, changing water into wine, feeding great multitudes with only a few loaves of bread and a few fish. Over the centuries these stories have either impressed or embarrassed those who heard them. Some would see them as evidence of Jesus' divine power, while others see them as evidence of people's willingness to exaggerate.

What can we possibly prove at this late date? We have no photographs, no newspaper reports, only the stories preserved in a few very biased accounts passed on by word of mouth for a number of years before being written down in their present form. Some modern Christians have suggested that the feeding of the multitude can be explained as a simple case of the generosity of one inspiring others. When the disciples asked what food was available, they would say, one boy offered the few loaves he had brought and perhaps others were inspired by his example to share what they had brought, and so there was enough for all. Perhaps. But that requires rewriting the gospel to deal with a modern prejudice against miracles. It also ignores some of the richness of the stories as they exist. Quite apart from the element of miracle, the stories are loaded with symbolism that might have been very obvious to the first-century Christian but is not at all obvious to us.

Some of these miracle stories about Jesus are obviously shaped by the stories told of other heroic figures. The story is told of the prophet Elijah, for example, that he once fed one hundred men with twenty barley loaves and had some left. All four gospels tell of Jesus feeding thousands with a few loaves of bread, but John's gospel specifies that there were five barley loaves. That can hardly be coincidence. A first-century world was far less concerned than ours about the difference between the ordinary and the miraculous, but was concerned to demonstrate that Jesus was a greater prophet than Elijah. Numbers also were more significant to earlier ages than to ours. We may prefer not to stay in motel room number thirteen and decide to get married on the seventh day of the month, but in previous times numbers had far more significance. The feeding of the five thousand, for example, took place on the Jewish side of Galilee and involves five loaves and twelve baskets, while the feeding of the four thousand took place on the Gentile side of the lake and involved four loaves and seven baskets. First-century Christians would have known that important numbers for Judaism were the five books of the Law and the twelve tribes of Israel, while the Gentiles, spread to the four corners of the earth, were traditionally thought to be divided among seventy nations. The telling of these stories, then, may have less to do with the miraculous element than with portraying Jesus as a great prophet and the lesson that Jesus cared for and fed Jew and Gentile alike. To worry about what could actually have happened may be to miss the point the gospel is making. We need to be careful about asking twenty-first-century questions about a story that provides first-century answers.

So, too, with the other miracle stories. We may imagine that frightened disciples in the dark saw something that looked like Jesus moving across the waves and that the disciples felt so much safer after they woke Jesus up that the storm no longer frightened them—or we can study the Old Testament references to God treading on the waves and stilling the storm. Then we can ask ourselves whether these stories are designed to tell us what Jesus did, or who Jesus is. In any event, we can be certain that there is no way now to prove what happened and therefore the stories cannot prove to us who Jesus is. They can, however, help us to understand the first-century viewpoint and the claims these stories were making. They do tell us about a Jesus who cared for people's basic needs when they were hungry and who could calm their fears when they seemed overwhelmed. Those lessons remain important.

Teaching

Jesus was also a teacher. All the gospels agree that he often used parables—short stories that illustrated his point. Some of those parables have become so well known they have helped change the way societies function and the way human beings act, whether they are Christian or not. Legislatures enact "Good Samaritan" laws to deal with those who ignore the needs of others.

Mark's gospel includes the fewest accounts of teaching; Mark is more interested in actions that speak louder than words. Matthew's gospel gives Jesus' teaching in long sermons, such as the famous Sermon on the Mount. John's gospel centers Jesus' teaching on particular events, such as a healing that leads to a long discourse. No one can doubt that Jesus was an eloquent teacher. He drew such crowds that he had to get into a boat and go out on the water to teach a crowd on the shore. He had to find ways to escape the crowds occasionally for time with the chosen inner circle and to have solitude for prayer. When the authorities sent solders to arrest Jesus, it is reported that they came back saying, "Never did anyone speak as this man speaks." Many who would not call themselves Christians will freely acknowledge that Jesus was one of the world's great teachers. But there have been other great teachers, from Plato and Aristotle to Thomas Aquinas and Ralph Waldo Emerson. Is there anything in the teaching of Jesus that is unique? One of the most controversial questions about Jesus is whether he claimed to be unique himself. There are certainly aspects of his teaching that need to be looked at carefully in this respect.

Who Was Jesus?

First, there seem to be no direct claims that Jesus was the Messiah. There are stories in the gospels of people possessed by evil spirits who identify Jesus as "the Holy One of God," but Jesus never says this directly of himself. At a turning point in Mark's gospel, Peter tells Jesus that he is the Messiah and Jesus does not deny it, but tells the disciples to tell no one.

More directly, in the story of Jesus walking on water, Jesus says to the fearful disciples, "It is I; do not be afraid." The phrase translated, "It is I," however, is literally two words: "I am." The words echo what God told Moses when Moses asked God's name. God told Moses, "I am." God said, "Tell Pharaoh that 'I am' has sent you." Again, in John's gospel, Jesus repeats the phrase in various ways. He says, "I am the light of the world; I am the bread of life; I am the way, the truth, and the life." These words would seem to identify Jesus with God in a special way.

The most astounding claim, however, is made in a way that might well escape notice. The Bible can be read like any book, but it needs to be read also with great care and thoughtfulness. Ponder, for example, what Jesus is doing in the Sermon on the Mount when he begins to quote the Old Testament and then to overrule it. Jesus said:

> You have heard that it was said, "An eye for an eye and a tooth for a tooth." But I say to you, Do not resist an evildoer. But if anyone strikes you on the right cheek, turn the other also. . . .
>
> You have heard that it was said, "You shall love your neighbor and hate your enemy." But I say to you, Love your enemies and pray for those who persecute you, so that you may be children of your Father in heaven.
> (Matthew 5:38–39, 43–44)

Six times in a row Jesus cites the Law of Moses, the central standard of the Jewish law—and overrules it. "Moses said . . . but I say. . . . " Early in his ministry, people began to marvel at the way Jesus taught "with authority." But what is his authority to overrule the law God gave Moses? The Jewish authorities quite rightly saw that this is either blasphemy or Jesus is speaking with the authority of God. Who can do that except God?

The authorities, therefore, concluded that Jesus was not only a blasphemer but a dangerous one, drawing people away from them and the established traditions and religious institutions. Under Roman occupation, however, the Jewish authorities could not put someone to death, so their solution was to accuse Jesus of threatening Roman authority and thus to let the Romans deal with him for them. The Romans obliged, but in so doing made the cross—their favorite means of imposing the death penalty—the symbol of a fast-spreading faith that claimed Jesus had risen from the grave.

Resurrection

Ultimately, Christianity depends on a claim some have always tried to avoid for its sheer improbability: that God raised Jesus from death, that the tomb was empty on the third day. Paul could not be clearer on the subject when he asserts, "If there is no resurrection of the dead, then Christ has not been raised; and if Christ has not been raised, then our proclamation has been in vain and your faith has been in vain" (1 Corinthians 15:13–14).

There are, indeed, versions of Christianity that try to settle for less, but they wind up being something less than the faith that spread out from Palestine to survive the Roman Empire and find followers in every continent. That gospel is inevitably centered on the resurrection. The resurrection of Jesus is the ultimate statement of God's purpose for human life: death is not the end, God made us for eternal life.

And yet when we look at the gospel stories of resurrection, the variations in this central story we find there can leave us confused. The oldest version of the oldest gospel, the Gospel of Mark, speaks only of an empty tomb and women running away in confusion. Luke, on the other hand, tells of "two men in shining clothes" who told the women that Jesus was risen; Matthew tells of an angel with that message; John speaks of two angels. Other details of the story differ as well. What do we make of these discrepancies? Would it not be stranger if all the accounts were exactly the same? After John F. Kennedy was shot in Dallas, some reported one shot and others two. Some believed a shot came from a "grassy knoll" while others believed that a shot or shots came only from the warehouse. At a time of great stress and shock, memories inevitably vary. The essential proclamation of the gospel, however, is unanimous in saying the tomb was empty and Jesus had risen from death.

But what does "resurrection" mean? The creeds speak of a "resurrection of the body." Many Christians repeat the Nicene Creed every week without noticing what it says, and assume that the gospel has to do with the immortality of the soul. That, however, is a Greek idea and not what the apostles proclaimed. If the gospel proclaimed an immortal soul, it would be no different from Greek philosophy and would not require an empty tomb. The gospel has to do with a risen *body*. But what is a risen body like? It is not simply a resuscitated body; Jesus' appearances to the disciples after his resurrection are an odd combination of material and immaterial realities. Now Jesus can appear and disappear in startling ways and yet he asks the disciples to give him food to eat. At Emmaus he vanishes when they recognize him in the breaking of bread, and yet he challenges the doubting Thomas to touch the scars on his hands and his side. What sort of body is it that can appear suddenly in a locked room and yet can break bread and be touched?

Paul attempts to explain the situation to the Corinthians by suggesting that "all flesh is not the same flesh" and that just as birds and fish and animals and human beings have different kinds of flesh so too the risen body differs from the mortal body. Again, he talks about the way a seed "dies" when it is buried in the ground and rises in a new form. So, he goes on, "there is a physical body and there is also a spiritual body" (1 Corinthians 15:35–44). But doesn't that bring us back to the something like the Greek idea of a soul?

The difficulty is that we are once again trying to find words from our experience to describe matters beyond our experience. We are forced back again to the language of analogy and paradox and negation: it is like this and not like that, it is like this and also like that. But nevertheless a fundamental and life-changing assertion is made: he is risen! It is not enough to say that although he died, his inspiration lives on. We could say that about Abraham Lincoln and Martin Luther King Jr. and Mahatma Gandhi. What the disciples experienced was so real they had no doubt that the world had been changed by this event in a way that no other event ever had changed the world or ever would. They staked their lives on it—and that is not something anyone has done for any other great leader who died.

The testimony of those who were there is that Jesus had truly died and been buried and then, beyond all doubt, appeared to them, lived with them, ate with them, spoke with them. On that basis they proclaimed that those who "die in the Lord" will also live with him, indeed they will begin even now to live changed lives and have no fear of death. This mortal body, Paul wrote, must put on immortality. So there is continuity and discontinuity: the body will be changed but not merely cast off to free a spiritual soul. Whatever is most real and valuable about our earthly existence will be raised and transformed. We will be who we always have been, only more so—just as the risen Jesus was who he always had been, only more so.

WHO IS JESUS?

There are two ways of answering this question: one looks at it more from our side and the other more from God's side. To put it another way, we can ask who Jesus is in relation to God, or we can ask who he is in relation to us. We will look at the first question in the chapter on the Trinity. Here we will ask who he is in relationship to us.

The "historical Jesus" lived, died, and rose again two thousand years ago. Today the "Jesus of faith" continues to be a living reality for millions of people in every part of the world. This entire book is an attempt to spell out the meaning of that relationship, but one thing needs to be said here. Many of the ways people set out to be Christian are too narrow in one way or another. They are not wrong, but they miss the fullness and richness and transforming power of the deepest relationship with Jesus.

First of all, becoming a Christian does mean entering a living relationship with a living Lord. Being a Christian has sometimes been seen as a matter of following certain rules or laws. Laws are indeed useful guidelines, but simply obeying laws is a negative approach to any relationship. Obeying federal, state, and local ordinances will keep most people out of trouble, but by itself it will not contribute much to the strength of the community. That depends on positive contributions, such as serving in the army or Peace Corps, taking an active role in the PTA, becoming a Little League coach, joining the volunteer fire department, going to town meetings, and being involved in some at least of the myriad activities that are part of the life of a community. So, too, keeping the Ten Commandments is a nice thing to do, but it enables one still to "pass by on the other side" when help is needed. Christians can go to church every Sunday, even serve on church committees, and still have a very limited experience of the full meaning of faith in Jesus.

A second pattern often held up is Jesus as role model: Jesus is described as the example we should follow. The difficulty with that standard is determining exactly what it means. Clearly it does not mean for most people doing what Jesus did: walking from village to village teaching and heal-

ing and calling followers with no place to lay your head—
let alone walking on water. Feeding multitudes is certainly
useful but, again, not for everyone. Even asking "What
would Jesus do?" has definite limits. Jesus never ran for office
as useful citizens today might do, nor did he raise a family.
Jesus often said, "Follow me," but sometimes he said, "Go
back to your own community." Jesus is indeed an example
to us in many ways, but he is much more than that.

The Gospel of John comes back more than once to a
theme that goes far beyond obeying rules or following an example, and Paul, in his own way, holds up the same teaching:
for them and for any Christian who hopes to experience the
fullness of Christian faith, the purpose of the Christian life
is union with Christ.

John explores this theme first in telling of Jesus' encounter
with Nicodemus. He told Nicodemus, "You must be born
again." Later, in discussing the feeding of the five thousand
with the disciples, Jesus told them, "Those who eat my flesh
and drink my blood abide in me, and I in them" (John 6:56).
And at the Last Supper, Jesus taught the disciples to think
of a relationship with him as something like that of the
branches to a vine: "I am the vine, you are the branches.
Those who abide in me and I in them bear much fruit"
(John 15:5). Jesus prayed to God for his disciples, "As you,
Father, are in me and I am in you, may they also be in us...
I in them and you in me, that they may become completely
one" (John 17:21, 23). Paul says the same sort of thing in a
different way when he says, "It is no longer I who live, but
it is Christ who lives in me" (Galatians 2:20).

The Christian life is, then, a life of unity in Christ. Baptism is the entry into that life and communion renews it;
Bible reading guides it and prayer deepens it. We are called
to recenter our lives so that our self is no longer the center,
but Jesus. Such a way of living is not acquired overnight. It

is a lifelong process and may continue still hereafter. Exemplified by faithful Christians in every age and place, it has changed the world—and can change every individual, deepening and enriching our lives and the lives of others beyond any expectation. When Christians grow into Christ, Jesus is present in them. If this book points the way toward that life, it will have served its purpose.

The Trinity

There are three families of faith that are monotheistic and trace their origins to Abraham: Judaism, Christianity, and Islam. Christianity is distinguished from the other two chiefly by two words: Trinity and Incarnation. Christians believe that God, although one, is also three persons and came into this world in the person of Jesus Christ. Each of these ideas is a paradox (see chapter 3): it asserts things to be true that seem to be contradictory and even impossible. Why do Christians make these claims, and what difference does it make whether we believe them or not?

FATHER

Before we can talk about God as Father, we need to say something more about the development of the idea of God in the Hebrew Scriptures that we identified in chapter 3. The Torah, or Law, the Psalms, the Wisdom books, and the books of the Prophets all struggle to hold together the idea that God cares for God's people. This idea speaks of closeness and familiarity on the one hand, yet is balanced by an increasing recognition of the full meaning of an omnipotent, distant, unknowable Creator on the other. In the Psalms we read both of the Lord who is our shepherd (Psalm 23), and of the Lord whose voice "flashes forth flames of fire" and "shakes the wilderness" (Psalm 29). In awe of such a God, the Jews ceased even to speak God's Name and only used an indirect title, "the Lord." While God was clearly known as a God who cared for and offered protection for God's people, as a father cares for his children, explicit references to God as Father appear only in three verses in the Psalms and a few passages toward the end of Isaiah.

First and foremost, however, the Hebrew Scriptures insist that God is One. In distinction from the various religions around them with their multiple gods and goddesses, idols and images, the Jews insisted that God is One and cannot be represented in any material form. Still today the *Shema* is the central creedal statement of Judaism: "Hear, O Israel, the Lord our God, the Lord is One."

In the New Testament, on the other hand, the idea of God as Father is central to Jesus' teaching and in constant use in Paul's epistles. Jesus spoke to God as "Abba," the more familiar form of the word Father, more like "Daddy" in English. Paul normally begins his letters with a reference to "God our Father and the Lord Jesus Christ." Although Jesus most often referred to himself as "the Son of Man" (which is probably simply a way of calling himself "the human being," a way to avoid making divine claims for himself), his followers quickly began referring to him as "the Son of God." So we have a new emphasis on God as Father and the new idea of a unique "Son of God." How can we make sense of these ideas?

SON

We have seen how the New Testament implies again and again that God was present in Jesus in a unique way. Jesus spoke with God's authority and seemed to have a relationship with God far deeper and more intimate than the prophets and teachers who had gone before him. In his epistles, Paul attempts to work out a way of understanding the relationship between Jesus and the Father. In one passage, he begins by exhorting Christians to be humble as Jesus was humble, but in order to show how humble Jesus was, he goes on to speak of the position that was his in heaven. Jesus humbled himself, Paul writes, for although "he was in the form of God," he "did not regard equality with God as something to be exploited." From that high place, Paul tells us, Jesus

> emptied himself, taking the form of a slave,
>   being born in human likeness.
> And being found in human form,
>   he humbled himself
>   and became obedient to the point of death—
> even death on a cross.

Paul then goes on to say that because Jesus had so humbled himself,

> God also highly exalted him
>   and gave him the name that is above every name,
> so that at the name of Jesus
> every knee should bend,
>   in heaven and on earth and under the earth,
> and every tongue should confess
>   that Jesus Christ is Lord,
>   to the glory of God the Father.
>   (Philippians 2:5–11)

These words reflect the language of the Ten Commandments that speak of the holiness of God's Name, the prohibition of worshiping images of things "in heaven, on earth, and under the earth," and the insistence that God alone is to be worshiped. Yet God, Paul writes, has raised Jesus to a place where his Name is like God's and he also is to be worshiped.

There is less complete agreement that the letter to the Colossians is Paul's work, but many claim it is, and it is certainly a very early statement of what Christians believed about Jesus. It is hard to imagine any more dramatic statement of Jesus' relationship with God than the one in that letter:

> He is the image of the invisible God, the firstborn of all creation; for in him all things in heaven and on earth were created, things visible and invisible, whether thrones or dominions or rulers or powers— all things have been created through him and for him. He himself is before all things, and in him all things hold together. He is the head of the body, the church; he is the beginning, the firstborn from the dead, so that he might come to have first place in everything. For in him all the fullness of God was pleased to dwell. (Colossians 1:15–19)

This is the picture of Jesus that lies behind the title "the Cosmic Christ." If "all the fullness of God" was present in Jesus, how is Jesus different from God? And how could the cosmic God be present in a human being?

Paul is far from alone in making such statements. The Gospel of John begins with a powerful summary of the meaning of Jesus for Christians that deliberately echoes the language of the first chapter of Genesis. "In the beginning," Genesis tells us, "God created the heavens and the earth." "In the beginning," John's gospel tells us, "was the Word, and the Word was with God, and the Word was God. He was in the beginning with God. All things came into being through him, and without him not one thing came into being." What or Who was this "Word"? John answers that very plainly and makes it clear that the Word was Jesus:

> The Word became flesh and lived among us, and we
> have seen his glory, the glory as of a father's only son,
> full of grace and truth. . . . No one has ever seen God.
> It is God the only Son, who is close to the Father's
> heart, who has made him known. (John 1:14, 18)

In other words, when God first spoke to create the world, that creative Word was Jesus and God has come into this world in him.

On the other hand—and there is always another hand when we are talking about basic Christian teaching!—in the same Gospel of John that so exalts Jesus as co-Creator of the world, we read that Jesus became weary on his journey, became thirsty, wept at the grave of Lazarus, died a real death, and was buried in a real tomb. If he was truly divine, he was also truly human. How is that possible?

In the early years of the church's life, no one made much of an attempt to answer that question—they just asserted that it was so. As time went on, however, the need for better answers grew, most particularly because some people began to give such different answers that it was hard to see how they could all be right. As long as Christianity was persecuted by the Roman Empire, it was difficult to come together to work out satisfactory answers to the inevitable questions, and different answers were worked out in different places. When the persecution ended, however, in the early fourth century, it was possible to travel more easily. As a result, people became more aware of the various ways the faith was taught in different places and the difficulty of reconciling some of them. Something needed to be done to clarify the message.

When the emperor Constantine decreed an end to the persecutions and then gave official recognition to the Christian church, he did so partly because he hoped that this rapidly spreading new faith might help him to unite his empire. He was as distressed as anyone to learn that Christians themselves were not united. Some said Jesus was truly God, others said he was only like God, and some said he was only human.

In the modern world, Christians might come together and debate the issue politely and go their separate ways, if necessary, with some degree of good will and toleration. The ancient world, however, was a different place and it had never occurred to anyone that faith and nationality could be separated. If you were Roman you should worship the Roman gods, and if you were Jewish you should worship the Jewish God. Jews had been stubborn enough to force the Romans to tolerate them, but once the Romans understood that Christianity was not the same as Judaism, it was fair game for persecution. And once the emperor had established Christianity as the faith of the empire, citizens would be expected either to become Christians or to keep a very low profile. But first, it was important to establish who was a true Christian and who was not and that involved either making peace among warring factions or else eliminating all but one.

Therefore a council was called in 325 CE by the emperor to meet in Nicaea, in modern Turkey, and decide: is Jesus truly God or only similar to God? Bishops came from all over the empire to decide the issue and when the shouting died down, it was decided that the winners were those who said that Jesus is of the same essential being as God. They drew up a creed that many Christians still recite every week, called, of course, the Nicene Creed, in which they drummed home as hard as they could the message that Jesus is "God from God, Light from Light, true God from true God, begotten, not made, of one Being with the Father." Balancing that is the statement that he "was made man" and "suffered and was buried," thus also defining Jesus as truly human.

So that should have settled it. In fact, it was only the opening gunshot in a battle that went on for well over a hundred years, yet still ended up with the Nicene Creed being affirmed as the belief of the church. Notice, however, that the creed simply states that Jesus is truly human and truly divine and makes no effort to explain it. How could it? That one person can be truly human and truly divine is a paradox: we assert two mutually contradictory truths because no explanation is possible. At the heart of the Christian faith is a mystery beyond human reason and understanding. But why should that be surprising? The God a human being can understand is not God.

It remains critically important to assert that Jesus was, as the creed says, truly God and truly human. Christians almost always tend to assert one more strongly than the other. It's hard to maintain a balance. We like to sing the Christmas carol "Away in a Manger" which says, "The little Lord Jesus, no crying he makes," even though human babies cry. Was Jesus not truly human? But how would we portray a Jesus who was truly God and yet completely one with us? Any evidence of divine knowledge or divine strength seems to separate him from us. No explanation is possible, yet we can still ask questions and try to find explanations. Christians have always tried to do that and still do. Some explanations are better than others, but the one that answers all our questions completely is almost certainly wrong.

HOLY SPIRIT

The question about who Jesus is, however, was not the only question the early Christians had to deal with; there was also a question about the Holy Spirit. Jesus had promised to send the Holy Spirit, but the disciples seem not to have asked what he was talking about. Then, fifty days after Easter, the disciples suddenly found themselves indeed filled with a new spirit. Now, instead of hiding behind locked doors, they went out boldly into the streets of Jerusalem and proclaimed Jesus as "Lord and Messiah." Jesus, Peter told the crowd, had received the Holy Spirit from the Father and poured it out on them. There already we have what was probably the first statement about the Trinity.

But what is this Holy Spirit? References to the Spirit and the Spirit of God abound even in the Old Testament, but there is little evidence that anyone worried much about what that might mean. Very late in the Old Testament, however, another term appears that does seem to reflect the idea of a divine being distinct in some way from God. In the Book of Proverbs, Wisdom is spoken of as a distinct, feminine being who warns and appeals and counsels. So we can see in the Old Testament the beginning of a more complex idea of God who was beginning to be known as Spirit and Wisdom, but insistence on the unity of God prevented further development.

In the New Testament as well, there is no real attempt to analyze this Holy Spirit that Jesus has sent from the Father. Yet there does seem to be a growing sense of a new and distinct reality in the lives of Jesus' followers. The Acts of the Apostles, it has often been said, is really the Acts of the Holy Spirit since the Holy Spirit is the chief actor throughout the book. The Holy Spirit comes to them, speaks to them, fills them, guides them, forbids some actions and directs others. In one critical passage, after a council has been held to decide on policy, the council states its decision in a letter that says "it has seemed good to the Holy Spirit and to us," as if the Spirit had been a participant in the debate. St. Paul spoke often of the role of the Spirit in his life and ended one of his letters with another Trinitarian phrase: "The grace of the Lord Jesus Christ, the love of God, and the communion of the Holy Spirit be with all of you" (2 Corinthians 13:13).

So there were three realities that Christians encountered, but what is the relationship between them? Paul provides one way of answering that question in his first letter to the

Corinthians when he says, "There are varieties of gifts, but the same Spirit; and there are varieties of services, but the same Lord; and there are varieties of activities, but it is the same God who activates all of them in everyone" (1 Corinthians 12:4–6). In other words, although we speak of Father, Son, and Holy Spirit and know God under these different names, we are always speaking of the one God.

TRINITY

Christians, then, from the very beginning confronted new realities that tested their Jewish monotheism as it had never been tested before. If God is One, how could it be that they had come to know God so fully in Jesus and, again, in the Holy Spirit? The question could not be answered easily, but eventually it would have to be answered. The answer they found was a by-product of their effort to understand the relationship between divine and human in Jesus.

The terms Christians learned to use to understand Jesus were "person" and "substance." "Substance" is probably the more difficult term, especially because it meant something quite different from what it means to us. They did not mean "flesh and blood." It might better be called "essence": the essential nature of God or of humanity. Christians used that term to identify the difference between humanity and God: God was of one substance or nature or essence and human beings of another. Therefore, to assert that Jesus was fully human and fully divine, they said that although Jesus was one person, the two substances of human and divine were united in him. If that was true, then they could go on to talk about Father, Son, and Holy Spirit as being three persons with one substance. Substance unites the three persons of the Trinity, but person unites the two substances in Jesus.

This is, remember, a paradox. It is something that no one understands—you are not the only one! And yet it must be said in order to come to any understanding of what God is like.

We can also use analogies. Some have said it is like a human family consisting of a husband and wife and child: all three persons are united in love. But in that analogy the persons are more distinct than the three persons of the Trinity are. It has also been suggested that it is like the relationship between memory, will, and reason in the human mind. But in that analogy the three functions of the mind are not really distinct persons. Still another analogy is with the reality of a sunbeam that gives light, and warms, and tans the human skin on which it falls. The heat and light and chemical energy are clearly distinct and can exist separately, yet they are inseparable in the beam of sun. So the two essential Christian dogmas (an authoritative belief or doctrine), the Trinity and the Incarnation, are each a paradox that can be understood better with the help of analogies, but are never completely grasped by any single analogy.

WHAT'S THE USE?

If we can never fully grasp the meaning of the Incarnation or the Trinity, why go to all the trouble of making these mysterious claims? Does it make any real difference in the life of the ordinary Christian? The answer is a definite "YES!" It makes all the difference.

Take first the dogma of the Incarnation, that Jesus is truly human and truly divine. What difference does that make to me? If it is not true, then there is a God and there is humanity but there is no direct link between us. We find ourselves in the position of the Deists of the Age of Reason who imagined a rather remote God who had set the world in motion and left it largely to its own devices. Many of the founding fathers were of that opinion and preferred to speak of God as "Creator" and "Divine Providence" rather than use more intimate terms such as "Savior" and "Redeemer." But if God has indeed come into the world in the person of Jesus of Nazareth and lived a human life and died a human death, then we know God in a new and very intimate way—and God knows us from experience.

Look at it this way: suppose I have need of assistance such as only someone very rich or powerful could provide, someone like the President of the United States or the chief executive of a Wall Street corporation. How can I get to that person? I have lots of friends I can consult, but they cannot give the help I need, and I cannot get to the person who can help. Human beings, in the same way, stand in need of help God alone can give—but how can we approach a distant God so holy we dare not even say the divine Name? One of the most critical passages in the Bible speaks directly to this issue when it says:

> We do not have a high priest who is unable to sympathize with our weaknesses, but we have one who in every respect has been tested as we are, yet without sin. Let us therefore approach the throne of grace with boldness, so that we may receive mercy and find grace to help in time of need. (Hebrews 4:15–16)

There are many technical terms Christians use to express this truth. Most often, Jesus is called our "Mediator" and "Advocate." Where there is conflict or separation, a mediator is needed. Where I am unable to speak for myself for any reason, I need an advocate. And now, whatever separation there is between human beings and God is bridged and overcome because God has lived among us. When I stand in need of help, God has a human face I can speak to. That's the difference Jesus makes. That's why the usual Christian prayer ends with the phrase "through Jesus Christ our Lord," or, "we ask it in Jesus' Name."

The Trinity is of equally practical and essential importance. The Holy Spirit comes into human experience as God at work within us and speaking through us. Paul puts it this way: "We do not know how to pray as we ought, but that very Spirit intercedes with sighs too deep for words" (Romans 8:26).

Interceding is very similar to the work of a mediator; again, it means acting on our behalf. So to overcome the separation between human beings and God, God comes not only into one human life in Jesus, but into each human life in the power of the Holy Spirit. We ourselves are easily tongue-tied when it comes to speaking to God, but God helps us find words because God is at work within us. So we might say that Christian prayer begins when the Holy Spirit moves us from within to pray, and Jesus carries that prayer to God the Father. God within us and God beside us unite us with God beyond us. God remains a distant and powerful mystery and our human sinfulness only increases the separation, but God has acted to overcome that separation and unite us again in God's love.

All human beings have some sense of this multipersoned God. Anyone who has ever been struck with awe by a sunset or the night sky or the birth of a baby or a work of art knows that God is not separated from this world and human life. Anyone who has ever experienced a sense of gratitude for the undeserved love and other gifts that have come their way knows that God is at work in this world. Some express this by simply saying God is in all things and all things have a divinity about them, and that is true but leaves us, as we said in chapter 3, with an impersonal God. When we come to some understanding of the Trinity, we have a way to understand this divine presence that is not simply a force or impersonal divinity, but a very personal God to whom we can respond in a personal way.

Sin and Salvation

Having come this far, we need to go back to the first questions asked in chapter 1 and look at them more carefully. It is true enough to say that we sense something missing in our lives and look for a relationship that satisfies us, but the sense of something missing is complicated. We also have a deep-seated sense that it is not just "something missing" but "something wrong." In the world around us, in human society, and most of all within ourselves, something seems to have gone wrong and to need fixing.

Look at a newspaper or the evening news or any number of websites and you will find reports of murders and riots and wars and economic disasters. The first headline seldom if ever says, "Everything Went Well in Washington on Wednesday." On a more personal level, few of us come to the end of the day with a sense that we have done everything we ought to have done and are completely satisfied with ourselves and our relationships. Psychiatrists make a good living listening to people's troubles and more and more schools, even elementary schools, pay a counselor to help children face the tensions and traumas of growing up, whether in a struggling community in the inner city or a leafy suburban ghetto.

Americans today have more comforts and conveniences than people have ever had, and yet there are enormous reservoirs of anger that clever politicians can exploit by focusing that anger on "Washington" or "Wall Street" or immigrants or taxes or other convenient targets—all of which have been making people angry for some two centuries no matter whom we elect. We may elect other leaders, but we still find ourselves dissatisfied. We try a new diet, a different vacation, maybe even a different partner; we go shopping for something we already have in abundance, check in with our psychiatrist, stop in the bar for a beer, or maybe experiment with a "controlled substance" to make the pain go away, but the dissatisfaction remains, the sense that something is very wrong, that "it ought not to be this way." Yet it always has been this way, and human beings in every age and every kind of society have sought understanding and remedies.

In chapter 1 we went on to talk about God as satisfying that sense of need, but we ought also to look at ourselves more deeply and ask what it is that seems so wrong and how we might expect God to remedy the problem. Christian faith claims that what is wrong is in us and that God in Christ has acted to set things right.

In many primitive societies and some modern ones as well, rather than look at themselves and their failures, people have looked for a god to serve who would set things right for them. Ancient Israel was surrounded by people who looked for help by making offerings to the gods. If the gods were more satisfied, people believed that they might give them better crops, more success in war, or more children to carry on the family. Twentieth-century societies tried to remedy the human situation with better social systems. Communism and Fascism were simply extreme examples of the human attempt to create a better world. Democratic societies have centered their efforts more on better schools and fairer laws, yet dissatisfaction indexes remain high. The God of the Bible suggests that we need to look at ourselves to locate the problem and then look to God for help in setting things right.

The Bible offers a one-word diagnosis of the human predicament, a word that often seems to be more important to Christians even than God. The word is "sin," and undoubtedly Christians have sometimes been too loud and relentless in asking people to confront its reality but, like it or not, it does need to be faced. What is it?

Sin is not the same as evil
We can begin by setting aside some things that are not sin: evil, for example. Evil may result from sin, but there are evils in the world that are not sin. The most obvious examples of this are natural disasters: hurricanes, earthquakes, tornados, floods, plague, pestilence, and famine. There is a constant temptation to assume that these things happen because we are sinful, that they would not happen—or at least not happen to us—if we would only obey God better. But no matter what sacrifices we offer or prayers we say, disasters come.

We can and do argue over the extent to which human misuse of the environment leads to climate change, but human beings do help create some disasters either by stripping the land of the forests that would absorb the flood waters or building homes in flood plains or areas vulnerable to fire or by trying to save money while building structures in earthquake zones. Human sinfulness certainly plays a part in many disasters and no prayers can save us from such folly.

Disease also is a disaster that is largely unavoidable. We can avoid a good deal of illness by better health habits, by exercising and not smoking and by avoiding large quantities of salt and fat in our diet. With progress in medical science we have largely eliminated small pox and polio and learned to control malaria and AIDS. We may be able someday to cure cancer easily. But death, like taxes, remains certain and the human body will deteriorate and die. Prayer can be effective in some cases, but not all, and there is no one-for-one relationship between our sinfulness and our sickness.

Jesus spoke to his disciples on one occasion about an incident that had occurred recently when a wall fell on a number of people and killed them. "Do you think they were worse sinners than others?" he asked. "No," he told them, "they were not." God, he went on to tell them, makes his sun shine on the just and unjust. If you are sick or a wall falls on you, it proves nothing about your sinfulness. You may get rained on, but many others both better and worse have had the same experience. So evil and sin are not the same. Sin may well have evil consequences and we should pray to avoid such sins, but there will still be evil in the world and prayer may not save us from it.

THE PROBLEM OF EVIL

Why bad things happen to good people is a problem wise men and women have wrestled with since the beginning of civilization. If God is good, why do bad things happen? Two possible answers are that God is not good or that God is not all powerful. Neither of those answers fits with the teaching of the Bible. One of the most profound and helpful meditations on the problem of evil is contained in the Book of Job in the Old Testament. All the evidence suggests that Job is a good man, yet evil befalls him. His children are killed and his possessions are destroyed. His wife unhelpfully suggests that he curse God and die. His "friends" suggest that he has, in fact, been sinful and should repent. Job rejects these possibilities and, in the end, listens to God point out that Job is far too small and limited to understand the ways of God. That will hardly satisfy the human thirst

for answers and understanding but it is, in fact, the best answer we can find. Once again we need to face the fact that
we are not God and cannot expect to see things from God's
perspective. There is, however, one aspect of evil we can
wrestle with more effectively and that is sin—if we are clear
about what sin is and what it is not.

Some things sin is not
Sin is *not* sex. As human beings of flesh and blood we are
strongly motivated to reproduce by sexual behavior and are
not always wise in our choices. We are prone to go disas-
trously wrong in our sexual relationships. We can and do
hurt each other by our sexual behavior, but sex itself is not
sin and the solution to sexual problems is not to condemn
sex. Christians have often seemed to make the equation between sin and sex, and have given the impression that the
world would be a better place if we all avoided sex. Unfortunately, it is not that simple.

Sin is also *not* things that are fun. Christians have sometimes set out to make the world a better place by eliminating
anything else that might be fun, like dancing and drinking
and even playing cards, since dancing and drinking might
lead to sexual misbehavior and playing cards might take up
time that could be used for prayer or Bible study. But God
created a world that can be enjoyed in many ways and gave
human beings the capacity to enjoy it. Joy can also contribute to healthy social relationships and joy can lead us to
praise God. Having fun is not necessarily sinful.

WHAT IS SIN?
The Greek word for sin puts it neatly as "missing the mark."
Isn't that the sense of frustration we have with ourselves: that
we never get it quite right? Sometimes we miss by a mile and
sometimes by inches, but we do keep missing and the result

is that our lives are at best unsatisfying and at worst a nightmare for ourselves and others.

The Ten Commandments provide the best summary ever made of things that are sins: dishonoring God, misusing our time, abusing our relationships, murder, adultery, stealing, false witness, and coveting. All of these are only chapter headings for a long list of sinful behaviors. It is not enough, for example, to avoid committing murder. Most of us are occasionally tempted in that direction but manage to keep ourselves under control. Murder, however, is not simply action that results in the death of another. Someone may jump out in front of our car when it is too late to brake, but we will not be convicted of murder because we had no motive to kill and no anger toward the deceased. Since there was no anger, there was no murder.

On the other hand, we may have a great deal of anger and no way to act on it. We will not be convicted of murder, but the anger in our hearts is sinful nevertheless. It warps our judgment and gets acted out in unhealthy ways. Also difficult to assess is our responsibility when a company we invest in makes defective products that result in injury or death. What is our responsibility if we elect representatives who create subsidies for American products such that third world producers are put out of business? No law defines that as stealing, but we may quite legally have taken the livelihood from another human being.

We might like to argue that we can hardly be responsible when we have taken no direct action to harm another, but the last of the Ten Commandments, the prohibition of coveting, clearly removes that excuse. When we are forbidden to covet, we are asked to control our natural instincts in a way that most people would find impossible. Paul himself confessed that it was this commandment that made him aware of his sinfulness. "I would not have known what it is to covet," he wrote, "if the law had not said, 'You shall not covet.'" But sin, seizing an opportunity in the commandment, produced in me all kinds of covetousness" (Romans 7:7–8). The Tenth Commandment asks us to engage in thought control, and anyone who has ever been told, "Don't think about pink elephants," knows how impossible it is not to think about a forbidden subject. Nor is it irrelevant what we think so long as we do not act; actions begin with thoughts and until we find ways to send our thoughts in better directions, we are all too likely to act out what we have been thinking.

Whether it be thoughts or actions, use or misuse of possessions and time, abuse of personal relationships, or allowing our thoughts free rein, the Ten Commandments are all too clear about our failures. But that is only the beginning. The Old Testament summarized the law with the two so-called "Great Commandments": "You shall love the LORD your God with all your heart, and with all your soul, and with all your might" (Deuteronomy 6:5) and "You shall love your neighbor as yourself" (Leviticus 19:18). Have we ever given our whole self to any good cause or really loved even ourselves, let alone our neighbor?

But that is not the whole story either. In the middle of the Book of Leviticus, a collection of laws on all sorts of subjects, is what is known as the "Holiness Code." Some of the laws in Leviticus are largely irrelevant today, such as: "You shall not . . . mar the edges of your beard" (19:27) and "Do not sow your fields with two kinds of seeds" (19:19). Other laws are about good manners, such as "You shall rise before the aged, and defer to the old" (19:32). Some laws deal with social issues that are still very much with us, for example: "When an alien resides with you in your land, you shall not oppress the alien. The alien who resides with you shall be to you as the citizen among you; you shall love the alien as yourself, for you were aliens in the land of Egypt" (19:33–34). Americans have always been troubled by that command, even though, like the Jews to whom the law was addressed, almost all Americans were once immigrants. But the Holiness Code begins and ends with an injunction that sets the bar at the top: "You shall be holy, for I the LORD your God am holy" (19:2). We are to be like God. Yes, we were made in the image of God and are called to be what God made us to be. We do miss the mark indeed!

If there were any doubt about it, Jesus calls us to that same standard in the Sermon on the Mount by saying the same thing in different words: "Be perfect, therefore, as your heavenly Father is perfect" (Matthew 5:48). We are to be like God, but we are not like God and we know it. Sin is very deeply ingrained.

It also needs to be said that sin is not simply a personal matter between each of us and God. Sin also has a social dimension. When I fall short, the whole community is affected. Even more important, the laws and customs that shape the community are shaped by my vote and my participation in the community. If some of the members of the community lack equal opportunity, it is not enough for individuals to provide soup kitchens and food pantries. Laws need to be changed to enable all to find work and to be secure when age or disability leaves them without resources. The Bible is very clear about that in its own terms. Reapers were ordered not to glean to the edge of the field so that those who had no fields could also find grain. Today it is business owners and legislators who need to take the same responsibility for the poor and disadvantaged. There are sinful societies as well as sinful individuals and the whole society comes under condemnation because of the greed and indifference of some. Jeremiah could proclaim God's wrath against a sinful society, but he also went into exile when that society was defeated. Where there is injustice, we all suffer the consequences.

When Cain in chapter 3 of Genesis kills Abel his brother and God asks what has happened, Cain replies, "Am I my brother's keeper?" God replies, "Your brother's blood is crying out to me from the ground!" Jesus makes the same point in a very different way with the parable of the Good Samaritan who goes to the help of the stranger lying beaten at the side of the road. The "neighbor" is the person in need, however separated they may be in nationality or ethnicity or social group. We are sinners living in a sinful society; therefore we come under judgment—and therefore God came among us to teach and heal and forgive.

RECONCILIATION

If there is one thing the Bible is clear about, it is that Jesus came to reconcile us with God. "In Christ," Paul writes, "God was reconciling the world to himself." It is further clear that that reconciliation is centered on the cross. "We proclaim Christ crucified," Paul wrote to the Corinthians (1 Corinthians 1:23), and to the Colossians he wrote that through Jesus "God was pleased to reconcile to himself all things, whether on earth or in heaven, by making peace through the blood of his cross" (Colossians 1:20). We use several different terms to talk about what God has done—salvation, reconciliation, and atonement are perhaps the most common—but whatever terms we prefer to use, what happens is that the burden of sin is taken away because Jesus died on the cross and because he died for us.

So sin separates us from God, but God in Christ has overcome that separation and Jesus' death on the cross plays a vital part in the process of reconciliation. What is less clear is exactly *how* that reconciliation takes place. Christians can agree that God was at work through and in Jesus to overcome human sin and reunite us with God, but Christians have never been able to agree on exactly how that happens. Why was it necessary that Jesus die for us?

Here again we find ourselves, as we did with the Trinity and Incarnation, facing a basic Christian doctrine and without final answers. Over the centuries, many possible answers have been proposed, but no one answer has been universally accepted. The human mind is not adequate to think things through when it comes to understanding God. We may, however, be able to rule out wrong answers and offer analogies in an attempt to get a little guidance on a vital subject.

Atonement through sacrifice

The language used most often in the Bible and the church to discuss atonement is the language of sacrifice. Sacrifice was a central part of Jewish worship. Portions of the harvest and of the herds were offered to God to renew the relationship between God and the people. The great festival of the year was the Passover when a lamb was sacrificed as it had been on the night of the first Passover in Egypt. These sacrifices were still being offered in Jerusalem when Paul visited it after one of his missionary journeys. Sacrifice served several purposes, but most importantly it renewed the people's relationship with God. At first the offering of sacrifice was a joyous community occasion, but gradually the focus shifted toward a more solemn character centered on atonement for sins.

It is this understanding of sacrifice that is central to the New Testament explanation of Jesus' death. John the Baptist called Jesus "the Lamb of God who takes away the sin of the world" (John 1:29). Paul wrote to the Corinthians that "our paschal lamb, Christ, has been sacrificed" (1 Corinthians 5:7), and the letter to the Hebrews says that Jesus came "once for all at the end of the age to remove sin by the sacrifice of himself" (Hebrews 9:26). So we can think of Jesus' death as a sacrifice like the sacrifices in the Old Testament. As they took the best they had to offer but it was never enough, so God has provided a perfect offering that need never be repeated. But why does an all-powerful God require sacrifice in the first place?

Atonement as ransom
Closely related to the idea of sacrifice is the idea of Jesus' death as a ransom. Jesus himself is quoted as saying that his death would be "a ransom for many." This way of speaking assumes that humanity is in debt because of sin and, as Christian thinkers developed the idea, must be bought back either from God or from the devil. Thinking this way has an appealing simplicity and is picked up in a number of familiar hymns, but creates problems as well. Why, for example, would God need to offer himself a sacrifice in the first place or, if the debt is to the devil, why does the devil have such control over humanity?

Atonement by emotional impact
The ideas discussed so far are objective: God does something to change things. Some have also suggested that the point of the cross is to make an emotional impact on human beings, to say, "See how much God loves us; we must respond." A familiar hymn says, "See from his hands, his side, his feet, sorrow and love flow mingled down!... Love so amazing, so divine, demands my soul, my life, my all."

Certainly there is a subjective aspect of the cross, but then atonement depends on our emotions, and nothing that happened at Calvary changes anything unless it changes us. The claim made in the Bible is instead that God has done something that changes everything, and that remains true whether we respond or not.

Atonement as victory

Jesus' death has also been pictured as a victory in a battle between God and the devil. Paul writes: "Thanks be to God, who gives us the victory through our Lord Jesus Christ" (1 Corinthians 15:57). The idea of a battle appealed especially to medieval theologians. A hymn still included in some Christian hymnals says, "Sing my tongue the glorious battle; sing the winning of the fray." Christians speak frequently of Jesus' "victory" over sin and death, and Easter hymns and prayers often use that kind of language. Again, of course, the question can be asked why an omnipotent God should need to battle against evil rather than simply eliminate it.

THE LANGUAGE OF ANALOGY

We have talked already about the use of analogy when we try to talk about God, as when we say "God is a rock" or "God is like a wind or a fire." When we talk about how God acts in this world, we have no choice except to use the language of what we know to say something about what is beyond our knowledge. So when we say Jesus is our Savior or Paschal Lamb or the Conqueror of sin, we are borrowing language to try to understand better what is finally beyond what human words can express. We commonly transfer words from one area of life to talk about another area. We say, for example, that someone is "battling cancer" as if they were engaged in a military conflict, or we say that a soldier "sacrifices" his life for his country as if an offering were being made to the gods. Language like that helps us understand something for which more accurate words are not available.

The Cosmic Christ

Finally, in the Book of Revelation, where metaphor and similes are used to construct a vision of heaven, we hear of a Lamb that was slain from "the foundation of the world." Of course, there were no lambs when the world was made and there was no sacrificial system, but we are asked to understand that Jesus' death brought into time and space an eternal aspect of who God is. Self-giving, without limit, is of the very nature of God. Jesus' death enables us to see with human eyes what God is like. God is eternally self-giving. This brings us back to the doctrine of the Trinity: it is of the nature of a triune God to love and to give. A triune God is one because the three persons are eternally loving and giving. The Father loves the Son and the Son loves the Father and they are both united in the love of the Spirit. The Trinitarian God freely chooses to create a world and human life out of an overflowing love. A unitarian God, on the other hand, can only be loving by creating a world to love and so creates that world out of necessity, not freedom.

The crucifixion, we need to understand, is not just about the human Jesus undergoing death but about the cosmic Christ revealing the eternally self-giving, self-sacrificing nature of God. All the analogies are true as far as they go, and help us to see the meaning of Jesus' death and what it has accomplished. Jesus died for us and for our sins. Like a king going to battle against our enemy, like a lamb being sacrificed for us, like a rescuer who reaches down to save us in trouble, like a stage play that moves us to deep sympathy and produces a resolution to change our ways—the crucifixion is all these things and much more. At the cross the eternal nature of God is revealed in a human being perfectly united with God. And because in Jesus our human nature is united with the nature of God, the separation caused by sin is overcome. Atonement is about exactly that: being united, made one. It remains only for us to accept that offering by responding in faith to accept what God has done for us.

Worship

Forgiveness leads naturally to worship, but many other things lead naturally to worship as well. A simple definition of worship is "the response of the creature to the Creator." It is simply the recognition of a relationship, as instinctive and inevitable as the response of the child to the parent. It is a turning toward the source of life in awe and wonder, in thankfulness and repentance, in joy and in praise. The man or woman who says, "I worship God best on the golf course," has something right: we do need some peace and a break from the usual routine. What's lacking on the golf course is a community coming together in a response of prayer and praise to the God revealed to us in Jesus Christ. The golf course may be a place to begin, but it will not take most of us very far along the road to a saving relationship with God in Christ that can change our lives and our world.

All of us find substitutes for real worship in an attempt to satisfy our natural need for God without committing ourselves to the real thing. Many of these substitutes for God are good and worthwhile activities. Concerts, whether classical or modern, awaken a sense of worship in one way, and museums and libraries in another. A rock concert might even provide some sense of community. All of these activities can produce that sense of ecstasy (getting outside ourselves) that is an aspect essential to worship. They may provide a partial substitute for the worship we need and draw out some of our best gifts. But they are not directly God-centered. They are impersonal and God is not. They cannot fully satisfy the hunger within us.

It is also true that what many churches provide as "worship" is relatively weak stuff and often boring. Even worship that is an emotionally satisfying experience can, unfortunately, sometimes lead us away from God and toward a preacher's personal agenda. It can be a response to the wrong person. On the other hand, amid the multitude of voices clamoring for our attention, there are many churches that offer worship that can renew our lives and build us into a life-giving community.

Authentic Christian worship is, as was said earlier, Trinitarian: it begins with the Spirit moving us from within, it is offered through the Son, and is directed to the Creator. Christian worship is also grounded in tradition, offered in a community, and able to nourish and transform both the individual participant and the surrounding society.

TRADITION: THE JEWISH INHERITANCE

The patterns of Christian worship come, quite naturally, from Christianity's Jewish roots. The first act of worship spoken of in the Bible is the offering made by Cain and Abel from the result of their labor. The Bible makes no attempt to explain why Cain and Abel felt moved to offer sacrifice; it simply reports it as a normal human activity. Such offering, or "sacrifice," continued to be a central aspect of Jewish worship throughout the Old Testament and was still being offered in New Testament times. A significant part of the Old Testament is taken up with instructions as to how this worship is to be offered. Increasingly, as was noted in the last chapter, the offering of sacrifice moved away from its original communal nature and joyous character and centered more on the individual offering in repentance for sin. As time went by, the offering of sacrifice was also limited more and more to the temple in Jerusalem.

A second pattern of worship seems to have begun in the days of the Jewish exile in Babylon in the sixth century before Christ's coming. Separated from the temple where sacrifice was traditionally offered, the Jews in exile met on the Sabbath day to read from their history and from the words of the prophets, to hear teaching about those words, and to pray. That pattern continued after the return from exile and the gospels speak of how Jesus went into the synagogue on the Sabbath day and took part in the reading of Scripture. A central aspect of Jewish worship was, and still is, the annual Passover celebration that recalls the killing of a lamb and the sprinkling of its blood on the doorposts so that the angel of death would pass over the homes of the Hebrew people and leave them free to escape from slavery.

Christian worship followed in this double tradition of offering on the one hand and reading and prayer on the other. Like the Jewish tradition, it is centered on an annual celebration of freedom from bondage and death.

DEVELOPING A PATTERN OF CHRISTIAN WORSHIP

As the last chapter pointed out, one of the earliest ways of understanding the significance of Jesus' death was to see it as a sacrificial offering. Because it took place at the time of Passover, it was linked as well with the Jews' escape from slavery. Jesus himself, moreover, had placed the ancient pattern of sacrifice in a radically new light when he took bread and wine at the Last Supper and said, "This is my body. . . . This is my blood. . . . Do this in remembrance of me."

It is important to notice that this Christian meal, like the Jewish Passover celebration on which it is based, transcends ordinary "clock time" and places the participant in the event being commemorated. So words read by Jews at every Passover, the Haggadah, specify that "*We* were slaves to Pharaoh in Egypt," and in the Christian Eucharist it is as true to say that we are there at Calvary as to say that Jesus comes to us.

From the very beginning, therefore, Christians shared bread and wine in joyful recognition of Jesus' continuing, life-giving presence with them. The Acts of the Apostles tells us that after Jesus' resurrection and ascension the early Christians "devoted themselves to the apostles' teaching and fellowship, to the breaking of bread and the prayers" (Acts 2:42). The "breaking of bread" was apparently the first title of the service that has become central to Christian life under a variety of names: the Mass, the Liturgy, the Eucharist, the Lord's Supper, and Holy Communion.

At first this act of worship was continued very informally with no set pattern and probably, like the Last Supper, in the context of a community meal. The significance of the bread and wine seems to have been diminished by the larger meal, however, and to have become a source of some confusion and conflict. Paul scolded the Christians in Corinth, for example, for not waiting to eat until everyone was there. To avoid this kind of difficulty, the offering of the essential elements of bread and wine gradually became separated from an ordinary meal.

By the end of the first century, set forms of words began to be used, but even in the middle of the second century there was still considerable freedom in the conduct of Christian worship. One writer speaks of how they would gather and read from the words of the apostles "as long as time permits," and how the one presiding would offer up prayers "with all his might." But as time went on, the pattern became increasingly fixed until there were set prayers for every part of the service and a regular schedule of readings from the Bible.

Early Christian worship naturally preserved the two strands of worship inherited from Judaism. The first part of the Christian service, like the synagogue service, centered on the reading of Scripture, while the second part, centered on the bread and wine and recalling Christ's sacrificial death, brought with it memory of the Passover and the ancient traditions of sacrificial offering.

Unfortunately, as the pattern of the service became more fixed, the clergy took over more and more of the service. Finally, in the western part of the former Roman Empire, as the church continued to use a Latin language which most people no longer knew, the service became a clerical performance watched but not understood by the laity. Even the reception of communion, once the center and purpose of the service, became a rarity for lay people. They received communion usually only at Easter, and even then only the bread and not the wine.

This domination of the church by the clergy was one of the factors leading to the Reformation and the division of the church in the sixteenth century. In the confusion of that time and the following centuries, the centrality of the communion service was lost to many of the reformed churches so that the usual Sunday service became centered on the sermon. In the part of the church that remained in communion with the pope, the Sunday service, still in Latin, contained many elements of the ancient tradition of Christian worship but without significant participation by the congregation and without the balance provided by preaching that proclaimed good news.

WORSHIP IN A DIVIDED CHURCH

As a result of the Reformation, the Christianity that came
to America was not only divided over Christian teaching but
filtered through a variety of national and ethnic traditions.
Nevertheless, it is probably possible to speak of two broad
styles of worship: one primarily centered on preaching and
the other on communion. Both these worship traditions,
though claiming to preserve or recover the worship of the
early church, had in fact drifted away from it both in pattern
and purpose. What had once been a joyous sharing of life in
the risen Christ had become a solemn, sin-centered gathering
controlled either by the pastor in the pulpit or the priest at
the altar. What had once been a communal celebration became more and more centered on the individual members
and their sins.

The remnants of these ancient divisions are still visible in
the contemporary American church, but change is taking
place and divisions are beginning to be overcome. A generation or two ago, the typical Protestant church was centered
on the pulpit and included almost nothing to appeal to the
eye. Crosses and flowers and vestments for choir and clergy
were almost unknown, although the clergy would often wear
a black preaching gown. Communion was often offered only
quarterly or even less often. In many churches, Christmas
and Easter were not celebrated; indeed, it was forbidden in
early New England. Members of the congregations sat not
only for the sermon but also for prayers and hymns. Roman
Catholics likewise were offered little opportunity to participate in a service that was spoken always in Latin and, as in
the reformed churches, offered communion for lay people
only on rare occasions.

THE RENEWAL OF CHRISTIAN WORSHIP

The seeds of change in the Sunday services of the various churches can be traced back to the nineteenth century, but by the middle of the twentieth century an enormous movement of liturgical reform was gaining momentum, leading to a very different experience of worship today. The transformation of Roman Catholic worship was authorized by the Second Vatican Council, meeting between 1962 and 1965. Giving recognition to a growing desire for change and the recovery of the ancient understanding of the liturgy as a joyous feast, the Council authorized translations of the Mass into the language of the people and encouraged participation of lay people in various roles in the liturgy.

Churches not under papal authority were moving in the same direction at various speeds. Some had begun to enrich their services even in the middle of the nineteenth century, others only toward the end of the twentieth, but in many churches flowers and vestments are now widely accepted and communion is slowly becoming once again an ordinary part of Christian worship.

Much remains to be done, however, in the effort to recover the joyous community worship of early Christians. The fact that Christians still speak of the clergy as "the priest" or "the minister" shows that the biblical teaching that the whole church shares the priesthood of Christ and all its members have a ministry to the world is not yet widely understood. In the same way, it is still all too common to hear Christians speak of "taking communion" or "receiving communion," emphasizing that it is something received by the individual rather than something shared by a community.

In his classic book *The Shape of the Liturgy,* Dom Gregory Dix, one of the leaders in the movement to restore the Eucharist to its central place, called it "a thing of an absolute simplicity—the taking, blessing, breaking and giving of bread and the taking, blessing and giving of a cup of wine and water, as these were first done with their new meaning by a young Jew before and after supper with His friends on the night before He died.... He had told his friends to do this henceforward with the new meaning 'for the *anamnesis*' [remembering] of Him, and they have done it always since."

This most traditional pattern of Christian worship can be done "with an absolute simplicity" or with elaborate ceremonial, and yet it remains for many something strange and unfamiliar. It is also true that where the communion service is central, preaching is often neglected, and a service centered on preaching is still the normal form of Christian worship for many. A balance between preaching and liturgy, word and action, may be difficult to provide, but one without the other is incomplete. Human beings are shaped by language and they shape society with words, yet often "actions speak louder than words" and we need not only to hear but to act on what we have heard.

A similar balance is needed but often lacking between head and heart. Worship needs to involve the mind as well as the emotions. It is not enough to understand; indeed, our understanding will never be complete. Nor is it enough to "feel the Spirit" since feelings are easily manipulated. Renewal of the church is always needed and current renewal movements may help produce a better balance in Christian worship, but almost two thousand years of experience testify that such a balance is not easily found.

Part of the answer to the problem of balance is certainly to be found in the growing relationships between divided churches. As the inherited defensiveness and suspicion of other churches is overcome, it is possible to begin to appreciate and learn from each other. So, for example, Roman Catholics are giving more attention to preaching, and reformed churches are giving increasing attention to sacramental worship. Social change makes a difference as well. The impact of television shortens attention spans and produces a congregation more accustomed to receiving information through the eye than the ear, with the result that sermons are shorter and ceremonial more important. A rising level of education also means that more church members are able to take leadership roles in congregational life, which tends to reduce the domination of the clergy. A lower death rate and longer lifespan enable Christians to focus their attention more on this world and less on the next. The central focus of Christian worship may remain the same, but the way in which the community celebrates its faith is always changing and being renewed.

OTHER WAYS OF WORSHIPING

Although the Eucharist or Holy Communion or Mass remains the central act of Christian worship, Christians worship in many other ways as well. All the various types of worship are included in the Eucharist, but each has its separate importance also and a full Christian life includes many other forms of worship.

Prayer, for example, should never be only a "Sunday thing" but a daily aspect of Christian living. Many Christians never begin a meal without giving thanks for the food they will share and never end the day without a time of prayer, either privately or with their family or both. Many also begin the day with prayer so that they habitually provide four or five times of prayer daily. Some churches provide forms of prayer for members to use several times each day as they are able, while other Christians prefer to pray without set forms but with the words that come to them from the Holy Spirit.

As the Sunday service ordinarily includes confession and thanksgiving and prayer for others, so Christians in their daily worship include prayers that give thanks for the blessings of the day, intercede for the needs of others, confess their failures, and ask God's forgiveness.

Just as the Sunday service also includes reading from the Bible and meditation on it, so Bible study is an important part of the day for many Christians. Churches and Bible societies provide study guides with recommended plans for Bible reading, but many Christians simply start at the beginning of the Old Testament or New and read a chapter a day until they come to the end and then begin again.

Following still the pattern of Sunday worship, Bible reading usually involves meditation: thinking over what has been read and its significance for the individual. In place of the Sunday sermon, the individual speaks to himself or herself about what has been read and what it means. Bible study is also commonly done in groups. Almost every congregation has one or more Bible study groups that meet weekly, often in private homes, to read together and learn from each other. No individual alone can begin to see the richness of a Bible passage and the various ways it may speak to those who read it thoughtfully.

Meditation is often only a very small part of Sunday worship, although some congregations do pause briefly after Scripture readings and sermon to allow the Spirit to speak to each individual. But meditation has always been an important part of Christian worship and in recent decades has become an increasingly popular way of praying. One common pattern of meditation called "centering prayer" suggests that individuals spend twenty minutes twice a day focusing on a simple word or phrase and letting that word provide a center for a stillness and quiet in which the individual can simply be consciously present with God. Repetition of the "Jesus Prayer"—"Lord Jesus Christ, Son of God, have mercy on me, a sinner"—is a tradition in Eastern Christianity that has become widely known in the West, and provides another way of meditation or focusing the mind and heart on Christ.

THE ESSENCE OF WORSHIP

Worship is God-centered. It consists, as someone told the Spanish mystic St. John of the Cross, "in considering the beauty of God, and in rejoicing that he has such beauty." Worship in human practice, however, always has some mixture of self-centeredness. That is especially true of some kinds of prayer. Confession, for example, begins with a consideration of our own faults, and intercession for others is centered on their needs. Worship at its highest levels leaves all these concerns behind to rejoice in God alone. This sort of worship is often called mysticism, for it speaks of the absolute gulf between the created and the Uncreated, and accepts in awe and wonder the realization that God reaches out to us and seeks our response.

We see a number of examples of this response of awe in the Bible. When Paul had worked through his understanding of God's purpose as fully as he could, he knew he had only begun and exclaimed: "O the depth of the riches and wisdom and knowledge of God! How unsearchable are his judgments and how inscrutable his ways!" (Romans 11:33). The prophet Isaiah's words extolling God's holiness have been repeated for centuries at every celebration of the Eucharist: "Holy, holy, holy is the LORD of hosts; the whole earth is full of his glory" (Isaiah 6:3). And the Book of Revelation, the last book of the Bible, picks up that same theme: "Holy, holy, holy, the Lord God the Almighty, who was and is and is to come" (Revelation 4:8).

Every form of religion has at its center that same sense of awe and mystery. Whether it be the disciplined meditation of Zen Buddhism or the mystical contemplation of the Jewish Kabbalah or the Muslim pilgrim circling the black stone at Mecca, we see in these practices the same abandonment of self in order to give oneself wholly to the Absolute. A Christian would say that it is the same Spirit who is at work in all. The uniqueness of Christianity is the claim that the chasm between the Absolute and the creation has been bridged in the person of Jesus Christ. What all religions seek has been accomplished in him.

In the religions of East and West, and in all the major Christian traditions, there have been great teachers and practitioners of the mysticism that is the highest form of worship. Thomas Merton among the Roman Catholics, Rufus Jones among the Quakers, and Howard Thurman in the Baptist tradition are among the best-known spiritual guides of the twentieth century. But the popularity of Zen practices in America in recent years would seem to indicate that the Christian churches have failed to do enough to offer their members the opportunity to learn from their own tradition.

SACRAMENTAL OR SPIRITUAL?

One other continuing tension in Christian worship is between elements that might be called "sacramental" on the one hand and "spiritual" on the other. Some churches place a heavy emphasis on the use of outward elements such as bread, wine, water, candles, vestments, ashes, palms, and so on to convey spiritual content, while other churches deliberately minimize all such forms to concentrate on the spirit within. It is certainly true that the use of outward elements can become a distraction, but it is equally true that the lack of such elements results in a service lacking an appeal to the eye and ignoring the human need for outward evidence of inward meaning.

Human love is not simply about a physical relationship, but a couple in love will want to express that love in physical and material ways. So, too, because we are physical beings there is a natural instinct to use material things to express our love for God. God likewise, to express love for humanity, came in material flesh and blood. Outward expression of worship, especially of Christian worship, is appropriate so long as it doesn't become an end in itself. Times of silence and meditation without such forms is also a valuable part of a balanced pattern of worship.

The Christian Church

Almost the first thing Jesus did at the beginning of his ministry, according to all four of the gospels, was to choose disciples. If we read the rest of the story carefully, we notice that Jesus was constantly training those disciples. He taught them privately, questioned them to see whether they understood, and explained to them things they had failed to understand. He sent them out on training missions and "debriefed" them after their return. Although stunned by the crucifixion and resurrection of Jesus, they continued to meet together and deliberately chose one to take the place of Judas, the disciple who had betrayed Jesus to the authorities, in their leadership group. When the gift of the Spirit came, they knew what to do. They went out to proclaim the gospel and to tell those who responded that they should repent and be baptized. Those who were baptized, the Bible says vaguely, were "added to their number." But soon after that we begin to hear references to "the church," in Greek a word that means "called out" or "selected." As Abraham was chosen and called at the beginning of the story of the people of God, so God continues to choose and call leaders and members for the church.

Some people think you can have faith in God without the church. That's not the way the Bible sees it. God calls people into relationship not only with God but also with other human beings. "Organized religion" sometimes gets bad reviews, but disorganized religion would be worse.

Human beings tend to consider organizations a mixed blessing at best, but the gospel cannot continue to be communicated without them. Possibly we could learn about God from a book, just as we could learn about physics or chemistry or poetry from a book, but most of us need schools and teachers to help us learn and that requires an organization. Then someone needs to train and assign leaders, make a plan, adopt a budget, and all that kind of thing. The church, like any human organization, has been a constant frustration to its members, but unlike any merely human organization, the church has constantly been renewed in its faith and purpose by God, and has survived and expanded until, nearly two thousand years later, it has been planted in every continent and country. In one form or another, the church has drawn members of every race and ethnicity closer to their Creator.

BEGINNINGS

Christians often think of the gift of the Spirit at Pentecost as the beginning of the Christian church, in some places even calling it the church's "birthday." But the first Christians did not see it that way. The early proclamation of the gospel in the Book of Acts speaks constantly of the message God sent "to Israel" through Jesus of Nazareth. Paul agonizes over the failure of so many of the Jews to accept the gospel, but reasons that it is because of that rejection that the gospel had been carried out to the Gentile world. Nevertheless, he writes that in the end "all Israel will be saved" (Romans 11:26) and, even more tellingly, he speaks of the church as "the Israel of God." Thus the first Christians, many of whom were Jews themselves, instinctively saw the church not as a new thing but as the continuation of what God had begun by calling Abraham. The letter to the Ephesians says, significantly, that the church is "built upon the foundation of the apostles and prophets, with Christ Jesus himself as the cornerstone" (Ephesians 2:20). So the church, again, is seen as the continuation of something God had been doing in history for a very long time. In the second century a Christian leader called Marcion taught that the God of the Old Testament was not the true God, but that teaching was decisively rejected by the church as a whole.

The foundation laid by the apostles in the cities of the Mediterranean world was, in fact, laid on a Jewish base. Wherever the apostles went, they went first to the synagogues, which existed in Rome and Athens and the other major cities because Jews had not only been scattered there as captives after defeat in war but had also traveled there in times of peace to seek business opportunities. These synagogues had also laid a foundation for the church among the Gentiles. There were many in that world who had rejected the myths of the gods of Olympus and discovered in the synagogue a different faith that worshiped only one supreme God and called its followers to a higher standard of morality in the Ten Commandments. These Gentile "Godfearers," as they were called, were drawn to Judaism but seldom became Jews because of the demands made by the rite of circumcision and the difficulty of keeping the Sabbath and the kosher laws. Thus, wherever the apostles went, they found in the synagogue an audience of Gentiles ready to hear of a gospel that did not require these observances. Sometimes the majority of the members of a synagogue became Christians and it simply became a Christian synagogue; sometimes a congregation divided and a new Christian synagogue was formed. Either way, the foundation was in place before the apostles arrived and many of the traditional ways of the synagogue, such as government by a council of elders, simply continued in the new church.

YEARS OF PERSECUTION

The Roman Empire, like all the governments of earlier days, made no distinction between church and state and expected its citizens to accept its gods. The Jews had been so resistant to this demand that they had been made an exception, and briefly Christians were given that same toleration. But once the Romans realized that Christianity was not exactly the same thing as Judaism and was growing in a dangerous way, persecution inevitably followed. The Roman emperors were not consistent in their efforts to suppress Christianity, so there were times of relative peace followed by waves of severe persecution that made martyrs of thousands.

The effect of the persecutions, however, was not at all what the Romans were seeking. The threat of martyrdom assured that only the most committed would become Christians and new members were constantly drawn by the witness of the martyrs. By the beginning of the fourth century, Christianity had become so strong a force in the empire that a new emperor, Constantine, decreed toleration and soon thereafter established Christianity as the official religion of the empire.

As persecution had strengthened the church, establishment weakened it. Once baptism became "the thing to do," those who sought official approval quickly came seeking baptism. The result was a much larger church but one whose members were often not deeply committed to the faith. The same effect has been seen in recent years in Russia, Poland, and China on the one hand, where the church has been refined and strengthened by persecution, and the countries of Western Europe on the other, where the church has been weakened by prosperity and official indifference.

STRUCTURE

Jesus had trained a leadership group, but there is no evidence that he created a specific structure. The organizational structure of the church emerged in response to a need for order, under the guidance of the Holy Spirit. We read in the Acts of the Apostles that the growth of the church quickly led to complaints of neglect on the part of some, so a new group was selected to assist the apostles in administrative tasks, thus freeing them to preach and lead. The members of this first selected group had responsibilities for caring for the poor and marginalized in ways that later became identified with ordained deacons, a word indicating a role as servants. Elders (*presbyters* in Greek) seem to have continued quite naturally to provide the same congregational leadership in the early church as they did in the synagogues.

Other titles for ministries in the church that appear in the New Testament are bishop, pastor, teacher, evangelist, and prophet. The Bible also speaks of a selection process for some of these ministries that involved prayer and the laying on of hands. There are documents from a very early time that single out the three ministries of bishop, presbyter, and deacon, but it is not clear that a threefold ministry was adopted everywhere or what roles the different ministries played. The words themselves have been subject to much controversy. Bishop is also translated as overseer, and presbyter means elder but has become the word "priest" in modern English, so there has been considerable difference of opinion among Christians as to the meaning of these terms and the roles they should play in the church. Nevertheless, until the time of the Reformation in the sixteenth century there was a common pattern throughout the church, East and West, of area leadership by bishops and local leadership by priests. Other titles such as archbishop, cardinal, subdeacon, archdeacon, and many more have also been used to indicate various particular roles but were not usually considered distinct orders of ministry.

The abundance of these titles for ministries raises two important points. First, there is a difference between administrative or organizational titles and ministerial titles. An ordained minister, for example, may be the pastor of a congregation, chaplain in an institution, or teacher in a school, college, or seminary. He or she may be called pastor, minister, vicar, rector, dean, canon, professor, and many other titles, but these are organizational titles and are not given by ordination. In some churches there is a distinction made only between the ordained and the unordained or lay members; in other churches there are separate ordinations to the three ministries of bishop, priest, and deacon. Second, all Christians are called to ministry, although only some will be ordained to a specific ministry. As Paul speaks about gifts given for evangelism and teaching and administration and other such roles, so still today gifts are given without regard to ordination and lay people find ministries of many kinds, both in the church and in the larger society that the church is called to serve.

DIVISIONS

Jesus would no doubt be pained but not surprised by the existence of divisions among his followers. He prayed at the Last Supper that "they may be one, as we are one, I in them and you in me, that they may become completely one, so that the world may know that you have sent me" (John 17:22–23). The church has not yet come to that unity for which Jesus prayed. Even in the New Testament we read of fierce arguments between Peter and Paul and between Paul and Mark. Paul admonished the church in Corinth about the way they had formed parties claiming to be loyal to Peter or Paul or Apollos or Christ, and begged them to remember that only Christ was crucified for them. "I appeal to you, brothers and sisters," he wrote, "by the name of our Lord Jesus Christ, that all of you be in agreement and that there be no divisions among you, but that you be united in the same mind and the same purpose" (1 Corinthians 1:10). Such an appeal would need to be made only if divisions existed.

As the church grew, further divisions were inevitable. When the church found itself in different cultures and tried to speak to those cultures, it found itself divided by what seemed to be theological issues but were often simply cultural adaptations coming from the effort to speak in a way that was relevant to each particular place. Paul himself highlighted the problem when he wrote:

> To the Jews I became as a Jew, in order to win Jews. To those under the law I became as one under the law (though I myself am not under the law) so that I might win those under the law. To those outside the law I became as one outside the law (though I am not free from God's law but am under Christ's law) so that I might win those outside the law. To the weak I became weak, so that I might win the weak. I have become all things to all people, that I might by all means save some. (1 Corinthians 9:20–22)

Christians have continued to attempt to adapt themselves to their culture in order to speak more effectively to that culture, but the limits of that adaptation will always remain a matter of debate and controversy and will often result in divisions. Those who move with changing times will be accused of being "trendy," while those who resist new ways will be accused of being irrelevant. The unity of the church requires a willingness to be patient and listen to other voices, but that is not always easy to do on emotional issues.

During the early centuries the principal divisions took place primarily over definitions of Jesus' divinity. These seemed to be theological questions, but the divisions often followed regional lines and reflected local jealousies. The first great division in the church, between East and West, developed over centuries as the eastern and western areas of the Roman Empire fell apart. Travel became more difficult, separate Greek and Latin language worlds emerged, and finally, in the year 1054 the leading bishops in the East and West mutually excommunicated each other. The "presenting issues" for this Great Schism, as it is sometimes known, were such matters as the correct date of Easter and the proper haircut for monks, issues that could surely have been resolved with better communications.

THE REFORMATION

The second great division in the church took place in the sixteenth century and led to the creation of separated churches centered in Rome, Switzerland, Germany, and England. Significant issues such as the central role of faith, the proper role of the bishop of Rome, and the participation of lay people in worship were fought over but, again, the fact that the divisions came largely along geographical lines would seem to indicate that something more was involved. That "something" was the emergence of new nation-states representing the economic interests of their regions. In the medieval world revenue had flowed to Rome from all over Europe, but in the emerging modern world there were kings and emperors interested in acquiring some of that revenue to build armies and navies. If the church in Germany or England became separated from Rome, the money would stay at home. Therefore theological divisions could be exploited for economic gain.

The fact of division did, however, enable the churches in northern Europe to reform themselves in important ways. The same rising middle class that was beginning to play an important role in national life was attracted to churches that also offered them a larger role and spoke to them in their own language. Unfortunately divisions tended to exaggerate differences, since church leaders in the divided sections of the church found it more difficult to communicate—and often tended to assume the worst about each other. Since political and theological divisions often ran along the same lines, theological dissent also became political treason. When the pope sent priests to England to minister to the small minority that remained loyal to the pope, they were often seen as representatives of England's enemies, Spain and France, and therefore as enemies of the state they were executed as traitors.

AMERICAN CHURCHES

The story of the church in America can be found in much fuller detail elsewhere. What is important for this summary is to note that the sixteenth-century Reformation produced four primary streams in Western Europe: Roman, Lutheran, Calvinist, and Anglican. The Calvinist tradition came to American from England (Congregational), Scotland (Presbyterian), and Holland (Reformed), and took root initially in Massachusetts, the Appalachian Mountains, and Michigan. The Lutheran tradition came primarily from Germany and Scandinavia and took root especially in the Midwest and Upper Midwest. Anglicans came first to Virginia and then the Eastern Seaboard. Roman Catholics settled first in Maryland and then came from Ireland during the potato famine of the mid-nineteenth century and, toward the end of that century, from Italy, Germany, and Poland. Lutherans and many Roman Catholics, since they were not speaking English, were inevitably segregated at first in ethnic communities and continued to organize ethnic parishes until well into the twentieth century. All of these, as they came to think of themselves as Americans, began to realize how much they had in common with Christians from the other traditions and cooperation among the churches in many areas became increasingly common. By the end of the twentieth century, intercommunion agreements began to be signed between churches with sufficiently similar traditions, such as Lutherans and Episcopalians, Lutherans and Presbyterians, and others.

A second stream of more radically reformed Christians also emerged somewhat later, some with roots in pre-Reformation dissent like the Baptists, and others, like the Methodists, of later origins. Baptists and Methodists, in particular, took to the American frontier and organized revivals that sometimes swept the whole country. Many Methodist and Baptist churches have grown together with the older churches of the Reformation and become part of the "mainstream," while others have become more radical. The so-called "fundamentalists" come primarily from these sources and have been less open to ecumenical cooperation. Also to be noticed are still more radical groups with origins in the United States, sufficiently different in their teachings and practices to be well outside the Christian mainstream and, in some cases, though greatly influenced by Christianity, not really Christian in any recognizable way. These would include Unitarians, Mormons, Christian Scientists, Jehovah's Witnesses, and others.

WHAT IS "THE CHURCH"?

When Christians are asked, "What church do you belong to?" they respond in several very different ways. Some respond by naming a particular denomination such as Baptist or Episcopal, while others name their local congregation.

Very few are likely to respond by criticizing the question itself and saying that there is only one church. That is, however, the historic position of both the Roman Catholic Church and the Eastern Orthodox Church. The decrees of the Second Vatican Council, for example, speak only of the Church of Rome and group everyone else into "ecclesial communities" that lack the full character of the church since they are not in communion with Rome.

In fact, there is a range of opinion as to the meaning of the word "church." Some would see it as simply a voluntary association of individuals with common opinions, while others would see it as an indissoluble unity. The first way has a great appeal for Americans with their historic emphasis on individual freedom, and has probably deeply influenced even those in the most traditional churches. The second way of seeing the church, however, seems closer to what Jesus prayed for at the Last Supper when he yearned for us all to be one in unity with God and each other. It is also more consistent with the various images and analogies used by Paul in his epistles. Paul speaks of the church as a single body of which the baptized are members. He wrote to the church in Corinth that "we were all baptized into one body" and that we "are the body of Christ and individually members of it." But members of this body, as Paul sees it, are integral parts, like the hand and foot and eye and ear, none of which can say to another, "I have no need of you," so that in the body of Christ "there may be no dissension" (1 Corinthians 12:13–27).

Of course, we are back in the world of analogy here and looking for ways to explain something beyond the ordinary realm of our experience. In a modern family and community, we are taught to value our independence and self-sufficiency, but the New Testament sees it differently. The letter to the Ephesians uses the analogy of a bride and groom and speaks of the church as the bride of Christ. Here again, of course, our society teaches us to think of marriage as a dissoluble union, while the author of Ephesians (who may have been Paul or one of his followers) speaks of bride and groom becoming "one flesh" in marriage.

From a biblical perspective, then, the church is not a voluntary association but a living unity sharing in Christ's life and guided from within by the Holy Spirit. But if we accept this idea of the church, we have to admit that such a church is not a visible reality in our world. We see instead rival congregations and denominations competing with each other for members and all too often denouncing each other as inadequate—or worse. There are several things that can be said about this situation.

First, the church, as we have indicated, exists in an imperfect world. Its members are subject to all the pressures of national rivalries and economic insecurities, to say nothing of the impact of our education and upbringing, which constantly distorts our judgment. Christians need to understand that they cannot expect always to be right. They need to recognize continually the possibility that they are mistaken, and to be willing to listen to others.

Second, in the long span of history, the church (and the churches) has made mistakes before and undoubtedly will again. Nevertheless, it may be possible to speak of progress when we see conversations and increasing cooperation among the churches at every level.

Third, Jesus said himself that he did not come to call the righteous, but sinners. The church ought to include sinful and sinning human beings or it is not doing its job. If we are looking for perfection, it is not yet available. A perfect church is a contradiction in terms.

Fourth, we have already cited Jesus' prayer at the Last Supper in which he prayed for his followers "that they may be one, as we are one." That unity still lies ahead of us; we have not yet seen the church as it will be. The letter to the Ephesians says that "Christ loved the church and gave himself up for her, in order to make her holy by cleansing her with the washing of water by the word, so as to present the church to himself in splendor, without a spot or wrinkle or anything of the kind—yes, so that she may be holy and without blemish" (Ephesians 5:25–27). Another letter says, "Beloved, we are God's children now; what we will be has not yet been revealed. What we do know is this: when he is revealed, we will be like him, for we will see him as he is" (1 John 3:2). Like Jesus' prayer for unity, these verses indicate an ongoing process. We're not there yet!

Finally, it must be said that the church often *does* provide glimpses of that future glory. Saints and martyrs in every age inspire others with their witness. In our own day a wide range of witnesses, from Martin Luther King Jr. to Mother Teresa, have shown us what God can do in human lives, and it is in the church that such lives are nurtured.

THE CHURCH'S MISSION

Jesus selected and trained the apostles and they, in turn, trained and commissioned others so that the church could carry on its work. That task can be summed up in two words: *worship* and *mission*.

First, the church is strengthened and renewed by turning to God in worship. Worship comes first since without it the church would lack guidance and strength.

Mission, however, is of at least equal importance. The church that gathers for worship must also go out to serve. It has been said that "the church exists by mission as a fire exists by burning." Mission has sometimes been narrowly thought of as the work of bringing non-Christians to Christ, perhaps in distant parts of African and Asia. And mission often does involve crossing borders—but increasingly today we realize the borders may be within our own community. Mission may involve finding ways to communicate with someone next door who has no understanding of God's love because of background, upbringing, education, or experience.

Mission also involves serving the community in whatever ways are needed. Historically, the church has usually been first to provide schools and hospitals. In major cities from New York to Tokyo and Calcutta to London, the great schools and hospitals that exist today were usually created by the church. The soup kitchens, food pantries, and homeless shelters that serve so many Americans today are usually organized by churches.

Change and resistance

Mission can also involve working for social change. It is no accident that the church was deeply involved in the civil rights revolution in the 1950s and 1960s. It is most often Christians who bear witness for peace in times of conflict. But it is, of course, at exactly this point that the church's work becomes most controversial and divisive.

In the Sermon on the Mount, Jesus said, "Be perfect, therefore, as your heavenly Father is perfect" (Matthew 5:48). But what is perfection, and how soon can we reasonably expect to get there? It seems obvious that a perfect society would not need armies, for example, since everyone would agree on major issues. But what do we do in an imperfect world where we would like to be peaceful but find ourselves under attack? What do we do when another nation is taken over by fanatics who use their power to carry out genocide? Dietrich Bonhoeffer, one of the great Christian witnesses of the twentieth century, decided at last that it was necessary to attempt to assassinate Adolf Hitler. It seemed right to many Christians to support armed opposition to

Hitler, and more recently in military intervention in Bosnia and elsewhere, yet there are also historic "peace churches" that refuse to participate in their countries' armies and have been willing to go to jail rather than take part even in a "righteous war."

Corporate or individual responsibility

Another dividing line when it comes to Christian mission in our society and churches has to do with the role of government. Many Americans came to this country to escape oppressive governments, and the habit of resistance to government is very deeply embedded in the way many people think. Others look at the needs of individuals and the power of government and believe that it is perfectly appropriate to use the government for social purposes. Few would argue that the government should not provide some sort of "safety net" for those in need, or that those in need should be left without any help. Churches and individuals can, of course, provide much help; soup kitchens and food pantries have become common in recent years. But few churches have the resources to provide long-term assistance or the counseling and training people need to escape from the welfare system. It is also true that the wealthiest churches are not usually in the areas of greatest need.

Finding the right balance between government assistance and church and private programs is not easy, but Christians do have a responsibility toward those in need. Jesus' parable of the Last Judgment tells us that judgment will be made between those who responded to those who were sick or shut-in or hungry or in prison and those who did not (Matthew 25:31–46). Christians cannot deny responsibility, though they can disagree as to how best to provide that assistance. The resources that God enables us to acquire are to be shared, not hoarded, and churches exist—among other reasons—to enable that sharing to happen.

SUMMARY

The church exists to join Christians together in a living unity to worship God, serve God, and make God known. The divisions in the church are evidence that the gospel is reaching people already deeply divided by background and upbringing and education and interests, to say nothing of race and language and culture. If the church were not divided, it would be evidence that the church is not reaching out across these divisions. Overcoming such deep divisions is not easy, but the church exists, in part, at least, for that purpose and can never dismiss other Christians as simply wrong-headed. We need to listen to each other and work constantly to find the unity that is God's will for us.

Being a Christian

After all this discussion of God and the church, we need to look for answers to one last but vital question: *What does it mean for me?* The apostle Paul's letters ordinarily have two sections: first he talks about the gospel, and then he talks about the consequences. Similarly, we must keep asking the questions that help us understand what difference our faith makes in our lives. How do we serve God in the midst of the constant challenges of our work and family life? How should we act in dealing with friends and family, with employees and employers, with our possessions? How should we shape our lives on a daily basis? How can we find the guidance we will need? Christians have always needed answers to such questions.

It can be very frustrating to search the Bible for answers to these questions because Jesus and the prophets and Paul, who might be expected to give us answers, are often intent on providing specific answers for specific people whose situations may be very different from ours. Paul, for example, had to answer the questions people had about eating food offered to idols. If you went out to eat with a friend and discovered that the food had been offered to a pagan deity before it was cooked for you, should you eat it? If you did, wouldn't you be acknowledging a false god? Eating the offerings of idols isn't usually our problem, but if you are a deeply concerned environmentalist and learn that the main course is the meat of an endangered species, what should you do? The situation is similar enough that Paul's first-century guidance might apply. Basically his advice was, "What you don't know won't hurt you." In other words, if your hostess doesn't tell you where the meat came from, you aren't compromised by eating it, but if she does, then it might be better to skip that course. Probably that would work also in dealing with the meat of an endangered species. Since it's already dead, it won't make a difference whether you eat it or not, but if your hostess tells you it's a steak from the last bison in the state, you are entitled to push the plate away and say, "Sorry, I just can't enjoy that." Paul seems to favor avoiding controversy and holding to principles while not pushing one's faith aggressively on others. So there is certainly guidance to be found, but it is not necessarily direct and different readers may interpret it differently.

A similar problem comes when we try to find guidance in the gospels. Jesus said to one man, "Sell all that you own and give the money to the poor, and come, follow me," but to another he said, "Go back to your own village and tell people what God has done for you." So one is called to leave his home and one is sent back to it. What is right for one person may be wrong for another. How can we tell what we should do in our situation?

START WITH THE BIBLE
Christians have a number of tools available to help them find guidance for Christian living, but the Bible is the easiest place to begin if only because it is so readily available. If you don't have one at home, you can find one in almost any library or bookstore, and it is available online in many versions. No better advice can be given to any Christian than

to read the Bible daily (see chapter 2). Find time at the beginning or end of the day or on the way to work or at lunch time or whenever you have a few minutes free. Bibles come in all sizes and some will fit in your pocket or desk drawer.

Make a plan. The best place to start is with one of the gospels, the story of the life of Jesus. Read a chapter a day if you can, but it might be even better to read a section of a chapter and take time to think and pray about it. Ask why the events in that day's passage happened, and what they mean to you.

Try to translate what you read into modern terms. The professionals have translated Hebrew and Greek into English for us, but they leave us with the task of translating ancient terms into modern. When the prophet condemns those who lie on "ivory couches," does that mean we may sleep on elaborately carved mahogany beds instead? When they condemn those who give false value for the shekel, are those who profit from exploitation of the dollar or euro included in that judgment? The Bible comes to us from a world two thousand years away and more. When Jesus talked about sheep and shepherds, wheat and weeds, he was talking to men and women who raised sheep and wheat for a living. Most of us have to translate such stories into terms more relevant to city people.

When the Bible says, "Cursed is the one who moves a neighbor's landmark," we need to think about what that means for us. When a farmer tries to increase his acreage by moving a landmark, that's stealing. It is finding a way to appropriate something that isn't his. What would be the modern equivalent? Would it be selling stocks that we know to be worth less than advertised, or claiming a deduction on our tax return for a donation we did not make? That kind of translation can be very difficult because emotions and prejudices prevent us from seeing clearly and making the right connections.

In chapter 4 we noted that Jesus reinterpreted the central commands in the Old Testament in the Sermon on the Mount, saying, "You have heard that it was said ... but I say to you. . . . " Jesus could reinterpret with authority as the Son of God, but we are not in that position so we need to be very careful. It seems also to be true that the gospel writers themselves "translated" Jesus' teaching to make it relevant to the people for whom they were writing. Mark tells us that Jesus said, "Whoever divorces his wife and marries another commits adultery against her; and if she divorces her husband and marries another, she commits adultery" (Mark 10:11–12). Yet under Jewish law, a woman could not divorce her husband so Jesus would have had no reason to say that, and the phrase is not included in the passage in Matthew's gospel dealing with the same story. When Mark was written, however, the church was growing rapidly in the Roman world, where a woman *could* divorce her husband. It would seem, therefore, that the writer of this gospel was expanding on Jesus' words to make them apply to the needs of his own culture. This puts us in very dangerous territory! If the Bible thus expands on Jesus' teaching to make it relevant, to what extent would we be authorized to expand on Jesus' teaching to make it relevant to our world? Fierce battles are waged between those who try to make the gospel relevant today and those who insist on abiding by every letter of the text—and every possible shade in between those extremes. At the least, we need to think carefully and pray about it, and discuss such problems with others. We need also to recognize that others of deep faith will not always agree with us and that Christians need to be patient and understanding of those who come to different conclusions. It is not usually helpful to denounce those who disagree with us as being "of the devil." The devil doesn't need our help in gaining recruits!

It is important to be part of a Bible study group if we possibly can and to learn from others. The perspectives and questions of others can remind us never to dismiss any part of the Bible as irrelevant and always to recognize the need to go beyond a superficial understanding. The whole Bible shows us men and women trying to find their way with God's guidance in a difficult world. Their solutions may not be the right ones for us, but when we ask why and how they attempted to follow God's will in their world it may help us find guidance for doing the same where we are today.

DEVELOP A PRAYER LIFE

God speaks to us through the Bible, but very often what we find there comes to us through the experience of others; what Paul wrote to the Christians in Rome is relevant for us, for example, but needs to be interpreted. In prayer, on the other hand, we approach God directly. Christians should find times for prayer daily and make it a habit.

Prayer, in the simplest definition, is "talking with God." It ought to be as many-sided as our conversations with friends and family. Often when we turn to God, we begin by asking for something—but that is not likely to be the first priority in a healthy relationship with God, just as it is not the best way to start a conversation with other people. Normal conversation with a friend might begin with "Good to see you; you're looking well" and then move to "thanks for your help with that project last week; sorry I wasn't more help" before concluding "but could I ask you to help me out again anyway?" So, too, in talking with God, a good sequence begins with praise and thanksgiving, turns then to confession and repentance, and might finally also include requests. Normal relationships also include a good deal of silence as we walk

together, sit together in a car or living room, or work together on a project. Meditation or contemplative prayer is
often thought of as something for people with highly developed spiritual lives, but it ought to be part of every Christian's relationship with God, just as quiet times together
would be part of any other personal relationship.

Prayer is something we often do alone, but we need to
pray with others as well. Some people are lucky enough to
live near a church where there are daily services at convenient
times; others may find a prayer group where they work or
in their neighborhood. Some prayer groups concentrate on
the needs of individuals, with prayers asking for God's help
in particular situations. Other prayer groups concentrate on
simply coming to a deeper knowledge of God and sense of
God's presence. Centering prayer has become a national
movement and groups often meet to practice that type of
prayer several times a week. Some churches have standard
prayer books that provide forms of prayer for use at different
times of day. These often include Bible reading and provide
a plan for reading passages from the Bible day by day known
as a lectionary. These forms of prayer also can be used both
by groups and by individuals.

Spiritual Guidance

It may be evidence of the increasingly secular nature of our
society, but the ancient practice of turning to a spiritual ad-
visor—sometimes known as a soul friend or spiritual direc-
tor—has become increasingly common in recent years. Such
a person might be a pastor, whether of one's own church or
another, or someone whose own experience is deep and considered enough to enable them to advise others. There are a
growing number of people, lay and ordained, who have received training in this area. It is all too common for Christians to make resolutions to pray regularly and read the Bible

regularly and so on and then gradually abandon the good resolution, either for lack of clear results or simply because something else comes up and we forget about our goals. That is why being accountable to someone else can be helpful. None of us can be as objective about ourselves as someone else can be, and regularly scheduled meetings with someone to whom we need to report can, in itself, help us stick with our program. Such meetings also give us a chance to talk over what has been happening in our lives, and to get some direct personal advice from someone who has the wisdom and maturity we need to guide us.

GO TO CHURCH

So far we have been talking primarily about individual behavior, but human beings are social animals. We cannot survive alone. Christianity also is first of all a way of life to be shared with others. We need to belong to a church.

In choosing a church or any other aspect of our spiritual life, one basic warning may be useful: Don't judge by your feelings. Sometimes going to church and saying our prayers and reading the Bible makes us feel good; sometimes it does not. That doesn't mean the prayers and other acts are useless or that we should only go to churches that give us an emotional high. Think of how a child feels when parents say "no" or when a teacher insists on hard work. The child may be unhappy about it, but will still grow as a result. Practicing scales isn't a lot of fun, but a pianist still needs to do it. Christian growth also requires discipline. American Christians have relied more than Christians in other times and places on the personal emotional rewards of revivals. But the highs are often followed by lows and those converted in an emotional moment may not follow through to develop a faith for every day. It is also true that God sometimes deliberately sends times of spiritual dryness to test our ability to persevere.

Lack of an emotional response to a particular church or preacher or spiritual practice may indicate that it is exactly what we need at that point in our spiritual growth.

Spiritual discipline needs consistency. We know we won't get paid for working at our job one day out of three, but only one-third of American Christians are in church on Sunday. It's true that we cannot earn God's favor, but can we expect spiritual growth from eating one meal out of three?

Prayer and Bible reading and spiritual guidance are helpful to Christians as individuals, but church membership is also a necessity. God designed us to depend on others. Having made a man, God said, "It is not good for the man to be alone" and created a woman and a reproductive process so that every human being would be part of a family and society. Families can be supportive at times and frustrating at other times, but it would be unfair to accept the support when it comes and walk away when it doesn't. It's not all about you, after all. It might be that the sense of frustration in your own life is intended to turn you out toward others. For your own sake and that of others, look around and ask what you can do to make a difference that will benefit someone else.

Churches ought to be inclusive. There should be young and old, rich and poor, people concerned for social outreach and people concerned for overseas mission. People ought to be able to find their niche, whether that be in prayer groups or as ushers or in the choir. All are needed to build up the body of Christ. Paul talks about the various gifts the Spirit pours out on the church, enabling some to be teachers and some to be administrators and some to be evangelists. Each contributes to the common life. We may be tone-deaf ourselves, but a choir and music program enrich the church's worship and build up the community's life. It may not be our thing, but we support it for its value to others. Ideally we will find support for our own concerns and be able to accomplish more together with them than we could ever have done alone. Whatever our gift may be, we are likely to find others with similar interests who will work with us in a church that draws a wide variety of people. We will also be challenged to grow by people whose lives and interests are different from our own.

CHRISTIAN BEHAVIOR

Faith in God is supposed to make a difference in the way we live. The first and easiest way to act out our faith is by joining with other church members in a common project. Individual congregations will have different priorities depending partly on location and partly on the leadership of people with specific concerns. It is easier and more important to sponsor a food pantry in a city neighborhood than in a wealthy suburb, but some suburban parishes make an enormous difference because a few people commit themselves to such a project and draw others in to work with them. Similarly, some congregations make their priority a clinic in Nigeria or a hospital in Haiti and make it come alive through exchange visits and frequent publicity in the church newsletter and bulletin board. Such projects, if they are worthwhile at all, help not only those they serve but those who do the serving. Participants in such projects have a way to act out their faith and grow in understanding of the meaning of God's love for all God's people.

Nevertheless, all such projects and involvement may be less significant than shaping a pattern of Christlike behavior in daily life. We can sing in the choir on Sunday and stuff baskets for food pantries on Saturday, but then still snap at our spouse, exasperate our employees, and frustrate our fellow workers from Monday to Friday. If we have learned to see Jesus in the face of the poor, have we also learned to recognize that face in whoever sits at the next desk, checks out our groceries at the supermarket, or jostles us in the mall? A spiritual discipline of daily prayer and Bible reading ought to enable us to keep our eyes open and see God in both the world and the faces around us—to see and to respond consistently with love and patience.

Here's something else that may be worth thinking about. A popular hymn some years back repeated the refrain, "They'll know we are Christians by our love," echoing Jesus' words to his disciples after the footwashing, "By this everyone will know that you are my disciples, if you have love for one another" (John 13:35). Christians will be known by their love, Jesus tells us. Yet unfortunately Christians are often known by outward gestures that are seen as showing off or pushing our faith on others. While there is surely no harm in saying grace or quietly making the sign of the cross as we ask God's blessing on our food in a public restaurant, we need to ask ourselves what making that sign before going to bat in a major league park or pointing skyward after hitting a home run says to skeptical viewers on television. Jesus specifically condemned the behavior of those who made a public show of their faith. It is far too easy for all of us to substitute acts of public display for acts of love. In Jesus' parable of the Last Judgment, he tells us that it is what we do for others that makes the difference. If our love is not visible, then no public show of faith will matter—in fact, it will probably only alienate those who see it.

THE VISION

From the very beginning of the story of God's people, there is a vision of a future toward which we are being called. In Abraham's case, it was simply a promise of a multiplication of descendants who would be as numerous as the stars in the sky. In Moses' case, it was "a land flowing with milk and honey." God often begins with specific material inducements to discipleship. Young children also are often promised candy if they do well in school, but the candy is not the real purpose of the work. If they practice only to get candy, they are unlikely to become great pianists. So God's people came to the promised land, but many of them never really understood why they were there. The learning process therefore continued. As we read on into the prophets, the vision turns darker and the prophets see a day of gloom and thick darkness, destruction and exile. Failures have consequences.

But as the story goes on, we begin to hear about a vision that seems to transcend the real world. Isaiah talked about a wedding feast that God's people will share, and although he specifies that it will be "on this mountain," it begins to sound as if he envisions a new world entirely. We are given a picture of a time when almost everyone will live to be more than a hundred years old—so old that they will all need to carry a cane (Zechariah 8:4)! More than that, the wolf and the lamb will lie down together and they "will not hurt or destroy on all my holy mountain" (Isaiah 11:6–9). The "mountain" is presumably Mount Zion or Jerusalem, and we are obviously not there yet. But the vision or dream is still renewed from age to age.

What will that world be like? Probably the English poet and preacher John Donne described it as well as anyone could almost four hundred years ago when he said in one of his sermons:

> In that heaven the moon is more glorious than our sun, and the sun as glorious as the one who made it. In this new earth all the waters are milk and all the milk is honey; all the grass is corn and all the corn is manna; all the clods of earth are gold and all the gold of countless carats; all the minutes are ages and all the ages eternity, everything is every minute in the highest exultation, as good as it can be, and yet superexalted

and infinitely multiplied by every minute's addition; every minute is infinitely better than ever it was before. Of these new heavens and this new earth we must say at last we can say nothing. For human eye has not seen nor ear heard nor heart conceived the state of this place. We limit our consideration to this: it is that new heaven and new earth where righteousness is at home.

And if we are going to a place "where righteousness is at home," we inevitably and rightly work to conform this world to that one. Again and again, nations and societies have been shaped to some degree by that vision. The Puritan settlers of New England set out to realize the vision when John Winthrop asked them to understand that "we shall be as a city upon a hill—the eyes of all people are upon us." A century and a half later, the leaders of the American Revolution created documents setting out their vision of a society based on the biblical vision that "all men are created equal [and] endowed by their Creator with certain unalienable rights," and they set out to "establish justice [and] insure domestic tranquility." But slavery and injustice remained.

Martin Luther King Jr. was very much in that tradition in his great speech from the steps of the Lincoln Memorial on the Washington Mall, though it might be called more specific and more practical than the words of the prophets. "I have a dream," he said, "that my four little children will one day live in a nation where they will not be judged by the color of their skin but by the content of their character." There have been many such attempts to translate the vision into political reality, but the vision is far beyond any of them.

The New Testament ends with one of the most dramatic visions ever recorded. As in Isaiah, the vision in the Revelation to John is an invitation to a wedding feast, but much of the writing employs a symbolism—numbers and angels and plagues and beasts—that no one can be sure they understand anymore. All too many Christians have tried to find literal meanings and have been disappointed. Toward the end of the book, however, are passages that need no translation:

> See, the home of God is among mortals.
> He will dwell with them;
>   they will be his peoples....
> They will hunger no more, and thirst no more...
> and God will wipe away every tear from their eyes.
>   (Revelation 21:3–4, 7:16–17)

The vision includes a city without walls where there is no more night and where the tree of life produces leaves "for the healing of the nations" (Revelation 22:2). It is a vision that seeks much more than individual comfort or fulfillment. It is a social vision in which people out of every nation and race and tongue are united in praise of God.

All these visions might be seen as various ways of conveying a very simple message: God has a purpose for human beings beyond the present world. The way to that world, however, lies always through the one we know. It is not an escapist message that endures this world for the sake of "pie in the sky." Someone has said that "the best kept inns are on the through roads." Those on the way to the vision have a standard by which to judge this world and are inevitably dissatisfied with the world as it is. It is those who are on their way to a better world who have always done most to transform this one.

That transformation is taking place week by week in the various congregations of the Christian church. That is where children are being taught that God is a God of love, where teenagers can gain a sense of purpose, where adults can hear a message that speaks to them and be nourished by sermons and sacraments that give them renewal and strength available nowhere else. The church is where our questions about life's purpose can find answers that have been welcomed and valued in every human society for almost two thousand years.

No one book can do more than begin to explore the full meaning of Christian faith, but there are churches everywhere that will welcome newcomers and help them find the next steps they need to take on the journey to which God calls us.

Questions for Reflection and Discussion

CHAPTER 1: BELIEVING

1. In this chapter the author explores the questions that often lead to believing in the divine, and the ways of knowing that contribute to our beliefs about God. "Two aspects of human life," he writes, "seem to be especially involved in this kind of knowledge: an awareness of our failures, and our sense of wonder" (p. 7). What experiences of awe and wonder have shaped your beliefs about God? What experiences of failure or limitation have contributed to your understanding of God?

2. Of the five traditional arguments for the existence of God described in this chapter, which ones are most convincing to you? Why?

CHAPTER 2: THE BIBLE

1. When it comes to the Bible, the author writes, people have to discover what authority it has for them "by reading

the Bible and reflecting on it and deciding whether it helps them to understand the meaning and purpose of life" (p. 20). What authority does the Bible have in your life? How does it inform your understanding of God?

2. What stories or passages in the Bible have been most meaningful and helpful to you? Which do you find confusing or even distasteful? How do you deal with those parts of the Bible that contradict or call into question the cultural values of your own family, town, or country?

CHAPTER 3: GOD
1. In this chapter the author describes a number of the images and analogies that have been used to talk about God over the centuries. Which ones do you find most helpful? Why?

2. If you were to write a creed about what you believe to be true about God, what words or images would you choose? How would you describe the creative being of God? the redeeming action of God? the presence of God in the world?

CHAPTER 4: JESUS
1. In this chapter the author writes, "To ask who Jesus is for us, we need to ask who we are and what our needs and expectations are, and to consider how these have been shaped by our upbringing and experience" (p. 48). How would you respond to the question, "Who is Jesus for you?" What aspects of your background and personality have been particularly relevant in shaping your experience and understanding of Jesus?

2. What aspects of Jesus' life, teachings, and ministry as they are described in the gospel accounts do you find most

meaningful? What do you find difficult to understand? How do you interpret the stories of healing and other miraculous events? What do they tell you about who Jesus is? about who God is?

CHAPTER 5: THE TRINITY

1. What analogies or images of God have helped you to understand the doctrine of the Trinity? Are some traditional words or images more helpful than others? What are their limitations and dangers when we use them?

2. The author believes that "all human beings have some sense of this multipersoned God" who is "a very personal God to whom we can respond in a personal way" (p. 73). How have you experienced God in your life as a personal, multipersoned God? Where do you see God at work in the world in a personal (as opposed to impersonal) way?

CHAPTER 6: SIN AND SALVATION

1. In this chapter the author asks a fundamental question people have asked for centuries: "If God is good, why do bad things happen?" (p. 77). What are some of the ways the Bible answers this question? How have you answered this question when bad things have happened to you or your family or friends?

2. The author writes that "sin separates us from God, but God in Christ has overcome that separation and Jesus' death on the cross plays a vital part in the process of reconciliation." He goes on to note that Christians have had a number of ideas about how that reconciliation takes place. How would you answer his question, "Why was it necessary that Jesus die for us?" (pp. 82–83).

CHAPTER 7: WORSHIP

1. The author writes that "worship is God-centered" and consists "in considering the beauty of God, and in rejoicing that he has such beauty" (p. 97). Where and when have you encountered worship that was "God-centered"? What have been the most significant forms of worship in your life? What made them meaningful?

2. How does your congregation balance the "spiritual" and "sacramental" dimensions of worship? Which aspects or modes of worship are you most easily drawn to? Which make you uncomfortable, or are difficult to understand? Why? What dimensions of worship are missing in your life now?

CHAPTER 8: THE CHRISTIAN CHURCH

1. The author notes that while Christians must "adapt themselves to their culture in order to speak more effectively to that culture," the ways we adapt are always controversial and the source of division. "The unity of the church," he writes, "requires a willingness to be patient and listen to other voices, but that is not always easy to do on emotional issues" (pp. 106–107). What issues have caused controversy or division in your congregation? In what areas do you find it hard to "listen to other voices"? How do you think the church should deal with dissent?

2. "The church that gathers for worship," writes the author in this chapter, "must also go out to serve" (p. 113). What do you think of when you hear the word "mission"? Where have you seen the mission of the church operating most effectively? In what ways have you participated in the mission of the church, such as in working for social change or the equitable distribution of resources?

CHAPTER 9: BEING A CHRISTIAN

1. What difference does your faith make in your life? How does your belief in God affect the way you live, the decisions you make, the relationships you have with others? What aspects of your life do you keep separate from your faith? Why?

2. How do you practice your faith and encourage it to grow? Where could you learn more about the Bible? theology? church history and tradition? prayer and worship? ethics? What concrete steps would you like to take in the coming weeks to nurture your relationship with God?